BREAKING BARRIERS
MY LIFE STORIES

Dr. Inder PS Gadh

Breaking Barriers

By Dr. Inder PS Gadh

Library of Congress Control Number: 2025908626

ISBN (Paperback): 979-8-9987496-0-5

ISBN (Hardcover): 979-8-9987496-1-2

ISBN (Kindle): 979-8-9987496-2-9

ISBN (EPUB): 979-8-9987496-3-6

TABLE OF CONTENTS

INTRODUCTION

After more than twenty-four years of service with the United States Department of Agriculture, I reached my full retirement age of sixty-six and decided to retire in April 2016. I had no clear plan for how I would spend the free time that now stretched wide before me. My wife was running a small retail business and, with a touch of humor, offered me a place to hang around, on the condition, she joked, that I wouldn't expect to be paid. I accepted her offer with a smile, knowing she didn't truly mean it.

Day after day, I made my way to her store, spending long hours helping out wherever I could. By evening, I would return home, pleasantly exhausted. This routine continued for the next three years. During that time, the business thrived, and sales soared beyond expectations. Eventually, my wife made the decision to sell it, believing the high sales volume would attract serious buyers. She was right. The business sold quickly, even before it could be listed.

With the store gone, I once again found myself at a crossroads. Weekdays now felt oddly open and quiet. The weekends were easier. As Chairman of the Board of Directors for a non-profit religious organization, I had a steady stream of voluntary work that kept me engaged. Still, the weekdays loomed large with unstructured time.

Then a longtime friend offered a suggestion that caught me by surprise. "You should write a book about your life," he said. "You've got a lot of stories, ones that could inspire someone." I wasn't sure I believed him. Part of me wondered whether my story was really worth telling.

"There are many folks out there who might relate to your journey," my friend continued. "For some, it could be a mirror of their own experiences. For others, it might serve as a kind of time capsule, something they can explore and compare to their present-day lives."

Still, I hesitated. While I had some experience writing technical articles and dissertations, this type of writing felt entirely foreign to me. I had never written anything so personal. More than that, I had always been shy about speaking of myself, let alone committing those thoughts to paper.

But time was on my side, and eventually, I asked myself: what do I have to lose?

That moment became the turning point. I decided to begin writing the stories of my life.

Then came another dilemma: what language should I use; Punjabi or English?

Born in Punjab, India, in 1950, I had spent over twenty-seven years there. Punjabi was the primary language of daily life, while English served mainly academic or professional functions. Many of the stories I wanted to tell were rooted in Punjabi culture, idioms, and customs; details best understood by those familiar with the region and its language.

Yet I also spent a significant portion of my life in Canada and the United States, where English was dominant and Punjabi influence minimal. I realized that by writing in English, I could reach both audiences, those born in Punjab as well as those born in North America. English would also make typing and formatting much easier. And so, for accessibility and reach, I chose English.

The stories in this book reflect a journey, my journey, from living in extreme poverty to reaching a point where I had everything I needed to enjoy a comfortable life, and attained the kind of name and recognition I could only have dreamed of in my early years.

I never set out to write a traditional autobiography. Instead, my intention was to share selected events that carried meaning, moments that offered a message, whether positive or cautionary, and could provide insight into the circumstances I lived through. For privacy reasons, I have chosen to use pseudonyms for some of the individuals mentioned throughout these stories.

The structure of this book follows the timeline of my life, without any specific order of importance or preference.

The frequent use of words like "I," "me," "mine," or "our" is simply to help establish the principal character of the narrative and provide clarity for the reader. Truthfully, having started life in a small village, unsure on many days whether there would be anything to eat, then going on to pursue every academic degree I could, and eventually arriving at a place few in similar circumstances could imagine, I cannot claim credit alone. I believe that a greater power was behind all of it. Whether one calls it God, Allah, Ram, Waheguru, or by another name, I am convinced that it was this unseen force that shaped the course of my life.

As I now look into the rearview mirror of my life, I reflect on the hardships I endured, the missteps I made, the risks I took, and the close brushes I had with illness and mortality.

Chapter I – My School Life

Homework Matters

I chose to begin with this particular story because it occurred early in my life and left a lasting impression, one that would quietly shape the foundation of my entire educational and professional journey.

At the time, I was in the fifth grade, attending an elementary school in Sri Ganganagar, Rajasthan, India. Ours was a small school, and being in the senior-most class meant that our teacher was none other than the school principal himself. Known widely as the headmaster, he had a fearsome reputation. Discipline was his highest priority. He kept a watchful eye on class behavior, assigned homework with precision, and expected nothing short of excellence in examinations. His punishments were legendary, and feared.

Students who broke his rules faced two main consequences. One was physical: a humiliating ritual we all called "becoming a chicken." This involved standing upright, then bending forward until your head hung down between your knees, arms wrapped behind your legs, grabbing your own ears from behind. In this position, the punished student would have to waddle down the classroom aisle, all while the headmaster struck their back with a cane.

The second punishment was even worse: being made to bring your parents to school the next day, only for them to be scolded publicly in front of the entire class. That particular humiliation was more than most students could bear. Many, when faced with the choice, would opt for the "chicken" punishment just to spare their families the shame. As a result, few dared to test his rules.

The school was about five to six kilometers, roughly three miles, from my home. With no affordable or practical transportation available, walking was my only option. My parents always made sure I left early enough to arrive on time. But truth be told, I didn't need much urging. I liked leaving early on my own. One of the main reasons was the game of marbles, a popular pastime among kids my age, especially those in my neighborhood. We played it with glass beads about half an inch in diameter. The game, known as Nakka Poor, was simple in structure but rich in excitement.

Each player either brought their own marbles or used real money to buy some from others. At the center of the game stood the "lead" player, who would start with a fist full of marbles. The rest of us would place bets by putting our marbles down on one of four spots, numbered 0 to 3, on a cross-shaped diagram drawn in the dirt.

The outcome depended on a bit of chance, almost like Russian roulette, but without the danger. Once the lead player opened his fist, we'd count the marbles inside and divide that number by four. Whatever number remained after the division determined the winning spot. For example, if the lead player had 11 marbles, dividing by four would leave a remainder of 3. The player who had placed their bet on the #3 spot would win and collect that number of marbles from the lead player, equal to what they had staked. The rest of us would lose our bets, but there was always the next round.

Most mornings, a group of us kids would gather in an open lot, usually one that was vacant, neglected, or enclosed by walls or other barriers. These spots offered just enough seclusion to keep us away from the watchful eyes of passing adults, especially parents and school teachers. We played for as long as time allowed or until someone ran out of marbles. Then, we'd slip the leftovers into our school bags and head off to class as if it were just another part of our daily routine. This became a near-daily ritual.

Over time, our little game began to attract attention, not admiration, but concern. Parents grew worried and started complaining to the school, urging the staff to intervene before their children developed a gambling habit. Still, in the absence of any concrete evidence, the administration remained reluctant to take disciplinary action against the students involved.

Then came a day when luck seemed to favor me. I won most of the marbles in the morning game and carried them all to school in my bag. The victory, however, didn't sit well with some of the boys who had lost everything, particularly one nicknamed Channi. Frustrated, he went straight to the headmaster and suggested he check my school bag. The bag didn't need opening, its weight and the clattering sound of glass marbles were enough evidence. I stood frozen, my body trembling with fear. I knew what could come next: the dreaded chicken punishment. But before administering any punishment, the headmaster paused. He asked whether I had completed the homework he had assigned the day before.

Luckily, I had. Being one of those students always afraid of his wrath, I had done it diligently. I handed it to him without hesitation.

Then he turned to Channi with the same question. Channi hadn't done his homework, and that made the headmaster furious. Without another word to me, he sent me back to my seat and ordered Channi to undergo the full chicken punishment. That day left a lasting impression on me. I realized how one simple act of preparation had saved me from punishment and humiliation. From that day on, I made a promise to myself: never skip my homework and never play marbles on my way to school again. At the time, I had no idea how far that simple decision would carry me.

What began as a small lesson in fifth grade, being prepared, taking responsibility, became a guiding principle in my life. It helped me earn scholarships, win academic awards, and eventually complete my Ph.D. That foundation paved the way for opportunities I never imagined: traveling the world, attending global conferences, and representing not just myself, but the United States of America and the United Nations.

Finally, I Got Through My Eighth Grade

After the partition of India in 1947, millions were forced to abandon their homes, fleeing for their lives as the subcontinent was split into two nations. Entire families left behind everything they owned, clinging only to survival. Many never made it, slaughtered in transit, caught in the violent chaos that erupted across the borders. My parents were among the fortunate ones. Along with their seven children, they escaped from what became Pakistan and made it safely to India. Three years later, I was born, their eighth child, into a life shaped by that trauma and uncertainty.

But survival was only the beginning. With no formal education, no financial resources, no job prospects, and no permanent home, my parents had to keep moving. Wherever they went, they relied on the kindness of strangers and distant acquaintances who offered short-term shelter or the hope of work. Sometimes we stayed a few days, other times a few years, but nothing was ever permanent. Each move came with new uncertainty, new challenges, and the constant weight of starting over.

I was in the third grade when a close family friend from Sri Ganganagar, Rajasthan, visited us in Punjab. He spoke to my father about the growing business opportunities in his town and urged him to move. Encouraged by the possibilities and trusting his friend's judgment, my father agreed.

5

The idea of moving excited some of us, especially the younger ones. For me, it meant my first train ride and a chance to see a new place. My siblings who were hesitant to leave behind their friends or jobs stayed back temporarily, promising to join us later. My only sister, already married and settled in Jalandhar, remained there but would visit us from time to time.

Once in Sri Ganganagar, my father wasted no time. With help from his friend, he started a modest business selling fabric. He would get rolls of cloth on credit from wholesalers, many of whom his friend had introduced, and carry them on the back seat of his bicycle, going door to door in nearby villages to sell them based on local demand.

At first, my father and one of my elder brothers, who had joined him as a business partner, did reasonably well in the fabric trade. But it didn't take long before the challenges began to mount. Fierce competition forced them to slash profit margins, and much of the merchandise had to be sold on credit, often to customers who never paid. As our household grew, so did our needs, and with mounting expenses, my parents found themselves delaying payments to wholesalers just to make ends meet. The wholesalers, in response, stopped extending credit. That was the beginning of the end. The business gradually crumbled under the weight of unpaid debts and dwindling inventory.

Then in 1965, my father announced that we would be moving back to Punjab. I had just finished the seventh grade. Though we didn't fully understand the reasons or know exactly where we were headed, the idea of starting over stirred a kind of strange excitement in us. We packed up once more, carrying not just our belongings, but also the lingering burden of hardship and the shame of creditors who had started knocking more frequently at our door.

Leaving Sri Ganganagar and putting distance between us and our creditors seemed like a path to something better, or at least less humiliating. That's what our parents assured us whenever we asked. Their confidence, even if shaky beneath the surface, sparked a sense of excitement in us. But while they focused on survival and starting over, my own thoughts narrowed to a single concern: which school I would attend for eighth grade, and more importantly, how many miles I'd have to walk to get there. No one had an answer. School logistics didn't rank high on their list of priorities.

Soon after, we relocated to a village called Barewal Awana, on the outskirts of Ludhiana in Punjab. What none of us could have anticipated was just how much disruption still lay ahead, especially for me. That year, I changed schools five times. I went from Ayali Kalan to Kokri Kalan, then to Miller Ganj in Ludhiana, back to Ayali Kalan, and finally to Gujarkhan High School in Model Town, Ludhiana. The last school was located nearly 10 to 12 kilometers from our home in the village, about 6 to 7 miles each way.

My parents couldn't afford to feed us regularly, let alone pay school tuition or buy a uniform that matched the school's requirements. These were some of the reasons I had to switch schools so frequently. Each change brought uncertainty, but it was financial hardship, not my performance, that dictated those shifts. When I arrived at Gujarkhan High School, the cycle finally broke. The principal, who had known my father for years and had learned of my strong academic background, welcomed me without hesitation. He assured my parents that the school would take care of everything, tuition, uniform, and supplies. My family wouldn't have to worry about a thing.

To make my journey to school easier, he even arranged for a friend to lend me a used bicycle. It was a simple gesture, but for me, it felt like liberation. No more walking long distances. No more missed classes. With that, and after five school changes in a single year, I finally completed 8th grade. Impressed by my academic record, the school offered to continue supporting me through high school, provided I stayed enrolled there. I didn't need any convincing.

Around this time, my father opened a small grocery shop in our village. Since my school was in the city, he often handed me a list of goods to purchase on my way home. He coached me on negotiating with wholesalers and managing costs. It was a kind of education in itself, one that unfolded not in a classroom, but in the markets and narrow alleys of Ludhiana.

In 1968, I completed my high school education. In my final year, I sat for the state board examinations. The results exceeded everyone's expectations. I broke all previous school records and scored among the highest, including 97 percent in mathematics. That triggered many local colleges including a medical college vying for my enrollment into their degree programs.

Bike Race – How Did I Miss My First Spot

In my final year at Gujarkhan High School, the annual athletic meet was in full swing. The school's wide grounds buzzed with energy as students gathered to watch or participate in various events. One of the most popular contests was the bicycle race. I always enjoyed watching it, perhaps because I cycled nearly 10 to 12 kilometers one way to school every day and knew well the physical toll it could take.

As the organizers called for participants and explained the rules, I stood in the crowd, simply observing. Then, a friend beside me nudged me, half joking, half insistent. "You ride more than this every day," he said, encouraging me to join. "Sixteen laps around this field is nothing for you."

I hesitated. Despite having played field hockey, volleyball, and soccer in the past, I never saw myself as anything more than a fill-in player, someone who was chosen to complete the numbers, not because of any exceptional skill. I didn't think of myself as a competitor, let alone someone fit for a race. But that day, perhaps because of my friend's push or some spark of confidence, I decided to enter.

Another reason I never took sports too seriously was the cost. I simply couldn't afford the expenses involved in joining a team as a regular player. Even for the bicycle race, I had always held back, not because I lacked the will, but because I didn't trust my bike. It was old, creaky, and the chain had a mind of its own. Every time I pedaled too hard, it would slip off, forcing me to stop and fix it, often three or four times on my daily ride to school.

Still, on that day, I decided to give it a try. If nothing else, it would show my friend exactly why I'd been hesitant in the first place. When the race began, I surprised myself by quickly falling into pace just behind the front-runner. I chose not to push too hard early on. Instead, I held my position and conserved my energy, planning to make my move in the final lap. By the time we entered the eighth round, I was only about eight or ten feet behind the leader, my legs burning but my focus sharp.

I felt no fatigue, only confidence. I knew I could overtake the rider ahead of me at any moment. But just as I was preparing to make my move, the race was abruptly declared over, and the lead rider was named the winner. Confused, I soon learned that the organizers had shortened the race to half its original length. Apparently, the announcement had been made before the start, likely while I was still unsure about participating and hadn't been paying attention. I had lost a race I could have easily won, not because I lacked the ability, but because I hadn't listened.

I remember standing there, wishing they'd run another round or that a second batch of racers would be called. I wanted a chance to prove myself. But that second chance never came. Instead, I walked away with a quiet but lasting realization: in life, you don't always get another try. It's a truth I carry with me to this day.

Chapter II – "Can't Believe I am Going to College"

"You Got a Telegram?"

It was the summer of 1968. I had just graduated from high school and was sitting at home on a charpai, a traditional bed woven with jute twine. In one hand, I held a hand-driven fan, slowly fanning myself, and in the other, a newspaper that I was only half reading. The heat was relentless, with temperatures soaring well above 100 degrees Fahrenheit. There was no electricity, no ceiling fan, certainly no air conditioning, only that handheld fan to offer some relief.

Our house was simple, just a single large room about 20 feet by 15, with a narrow veranda in front, roughly 20 by 8 feet. After acquiring the place, Bapu Ji, my father, had hired a construction worker to build a dividing wall inside the room using unbaked bricks. The wall stood about six feet high, splitting the space into two smaller rooms, each around 10 by 15 feet. A gap in the middle, about three feet wide and six feet high, served as an open doorway between the two sides.

The western half of the house, facing the village's main thoroughfare, had been converted into a small grocery shop that Bapuji managed. The eastern half, commonly referred to as the back room, functioned as both a bedroom and a modest kitchen. In one corner stood a queen-size cot, mainly used for sitting during the day or for storing bed sheets and pillows. The opposite corner, near the back door, was reserved for cooking. It housed a charcoal-burning stove, a free-standing floor cabinet that held dishes and essential utensils, and just enough space for my mother to sit and prepare our meals.

A small mat was laid out on the floor between the bed and the kitchen, where everyone would gather to sit and eat. At night, the entire family, which included my parents, my younger brother, myself, and any guests, slept outside in the veranda, the small backyard, or on the flat roof. This was the routine throughout the year, except during cold or rainy weather, when we would all find space to sleep inside, either in the shop or the back room, wherever there was room.

The roof was built with small wooden beams laid across three larger support beams and topped with layers of sticks and gaara, a blend of clay, sand, and water. Each year, before the monsoon season, my mother would coat the roof with a fresh layer of cow dung mixed with soil to seal any potential leaks. Since our house didn't have running water, we relied on hand pumps installed in neighboring homes for our daily water needs.

In the beginning, we didn't have a formal bathroom. To manage, we set up a small enclosure in one corner of the backyard using tin walls and a tin roof, which served as an emergency bathroom for the women in the family. There was no electricity in the village either. But a few years later, when electric lines were finally made available to the residents, I found a way to bring it into our home, though not by official means.

Drawing from what I had learned in a physics course, I figured out how to do the basic wiring myself and installed outlets to power light bulbs inside the house. With the help of a friendly electrician, I managed to connect our wiring directly to the power line from the pole outside, the same one supplying electricity to the neighboring homes. This way, we received electricity for free, while others in the village paid regular bills.

That arrangement worked smoothly for quite some time, until the authorities eventually discovered the setup and required us to comply with official regulations like everyone else.

One scorching afternoon in June 1968, the sun burned high overhead, as if trying to melt everything beneath it. The streets outside were deserted, no one walked, no one worked. Most had retreated to the shade, seeking whatever relief they could find. I sat alone inside, on the cot-bed in the back room, waiting for the sun to dip low enough to break the spell of the heat. Boredom weighed heavily on me.

With nothing else to do, I picked up the daily newspaper I had borrowed from a neighbor earlier that morning and began scanning the job listings once again. It must have been the second or third time I was going through them, double-checking to make sure I hadn't missed any opportunity that seemed even remotely promising.

In my final years at school, I had come across the novels of Nanak Singh, his words stirred something in me. They helped shape my conviction that the surest way to escape the suffocating cycle of poverty was through education.

Inspired, I often dreamed of joining a college like many of my classmates, especially those who had excelled in their board exams. I imagined spending my days in lecture halls, diving deeper into books, and distancing myself from the depressing weight of life at home.

But I knew the reality all too well. Our financial situation left no room for such dreams. I simply couldn't afford the college fees. The idea of attending college was little more than a beautiful, unreachable hope.

By then, my parents had already exhausted every possible avenue for borrowing money just to keep us afloat, so I knew there was no hope of them covering my college expenses. I was simply grateful to have finished high school. My father's small grocery shop barely earned enough to sustain the family, let alone support another hand. It couldn't offer me employment, nor was there any growth in sight. That left me with only one option, finding a job in the city. But even that felt like a distant hope.

With just a high school diploma, most advertised positions seemed out of reach. Many required advanced qualifications, and others were little more than formalities, ads posted to satisfy legal obligations before confirming candidates who had already been working temporarily.

I had just finished my lunch and was settling down for a nap when I heard footsteps and the sound of a voice drifting through the shop wall. As soon as the man began speaking in Punjabi, I recognized him immediately. It was Mr. Murari Lal. He was an elderly man who had taught for years at the village elementary school, the same one I'd once attended.

Over time, he had taken on extra responsibilities, handling basic postal and banking services to supplement his modest income.

As the village postmaster, Mr. Lal's responsibilities extended beyond mail delivery. He also handled pensions for retired military personnel and made routine rounds through the village, often stopping by homes just to say hello, even when there was no mail. That simple gesture served as a silent message: there's nothing today. It was a small act, but one that endeared him to everyone. But on that particular afternoon, Mr. Lal's visit wasn't just routine. He had come bearing a telegram, addressed to me. It required a signature or thumbprint to confirm receipt, which he obtained before quietly stepping away.

Not long after he left, several elderly women from the neighborhood entered our home, their faces marked with concern. In our village of nearly ten thousand, many households had sons or brothers serving in the Indian Army. Everyone knew what a telegram could mean. If a soldier had fallen or something serious had happened, the message always came this way, delivered formally and ominously, with no room for misunderstanding. Custom dictated that, before delivering such a telegram, Mr. Lal would alert nearby residents, giving them time to gather in quiet solidarity with the affected family. Their arrival at our home meant only one thing: they feared the worst.

The practice of following a telegram delivery was rooted in empathy. Neighbors, especially older women who stayed home during the day, would often gather to offer condolences, believing the message to be tragic. Many of them knew who in each family served in the Army, and when a telegram arrived, they assumed the worst. Typically, they'd begin weeping the moment they entered the home, mourning even before the contents were read.

That afternoon, a few of them followed Mr. Lal, as expected. But instead of crying, they wore expressions of curiosity. One of them, her voice tinged with confusion, asked my father, "Bhraa ji, we know you have no one in the Army. So why have you received a telegram?" We were equally puzzled. None of us had ever received a telegram before, and we didn't know what to expect.

From the back room, I had overheard everything. The woman's question stirred a wave of unease in me, and I couldn't sit still. I stepped forward, took the telegram from my father's hand, and opened it. My heart raced as I read. But instead of grief, I felt a rush of relief. It wasn't bad news at all. The telegram had come from Punjab Agricultural University (PAU) in Ludhiana, a respected institution not far from our village. It congratulated me for winning a scholarship to pursue higher education there, should I choose to enroll.

Punjab Agricultural University, Ludhiana, Punjab, India

Since the telegram was written in English, I translated it aloud into Punjabi so my father and the visiting ladies could understand. The news left them puzzled. This wasn't the kind of telegram they were used to hearing about. Just then, an elderly man began approaching our shop, catching the ladies' attention. With the promise of new gossip elsewhere, they drifted off, whispering among themselves.

After they left, my father turned to me. "Was there anything else in it?" he asked quietly.

"Yes," I replied. "To accept the scholarship, I must enroll in one of their degree programs within the next two or three days. That means I need to pay a registration fee of 107 rupees and 50 paisa."

I paused. The number hung in the air.

For a moment, he said nothing. His face tightened, not with anger, but with helplessness. That amount, equivalent to nearly thirteen American dollars at the time, might as well have been a fortune to us. It was more than we could imagine producing in a few days.

The old man, after a short exchange with Bapuji, left quietly. My father remained silent, unmoving. Whether he was overwhelmed by the burden or simply didn't know how to respond, I couldn't tell. But his silence said everything.

My father buried his head in an old ledger with a faded red cover, pretending to study its pages. But his silence had already told me everything I needed to know. There was no money. Not now, not soon.

I returned to the back room and sat where I had been before, but I wasn't the same. The thought of an afternoon nap had disappeared. My mind churned with the weight of a single question: How am I going to come up with that much money so quickly?

Still holding the telegram in my hand, I stared at it again. Until that moment, I had always believed telegrams arrived only with news of tragedy, mostly death. But that day, I learned they could carry other messages too. It was a strange kind of relief.

I stared out the doorway. The sun was beginning its slow descent, casting long shadows over the courtyard. From the distance came the splash of water, someone was bathing their buffalo in the village creek. Other sounds followed: voices calling out, the clatter of vessels, the soft grunts of animals. Children had come out, as they often did at dusk, playing in the open spaces, swapping stories, kicking stones.

For a moment, I felt the urge to join them, just to breathe the evening air and forget everything for a while. But when I glanced at my father again, hunched and unmoving over his book, I stayed seated. Leaving him alone in that silence might have only deepened his sense of helplessness, or worse, made him feel abandoned. I couldn't do that.

While lying on the cot-bed in the back room, with nothing to do, my mind wandered back to the stories my father often told us, stories from before the Partition, some of them so moving they could make one cry, and others that stirred deep pride. He spoke of the generosity that ran in our family, how he and his ancestors had donated hundreds of acres of land to help establish a high school for the community.

He also shared how, before he turned eighteen, he had joined a resistance movement called Jaito Da Morcha, which stood against the British Raj. The protestors faced brutal beatings, and many never returned home. In fact, the group was labeled the "Martyrs Group" even before they began their march. Perhaps his youth had spared him from the same fate.

Lying there, I began to wonder how a man like him, a man who had once stood for justice and served his country in spirit, had ended up so forgotten. How could someone who had sacrificed so much for others now struggle to keep his family afloat? The contrast was difficult to make peace with.

At some point, I must have drifted off. I only woke when my mother gently shook me and said the hot tea was ready.

Baba - The Guy with an Evil Eye

Baba, whose official name was Kala Singh, lived just a few blocks from our home and grocery shop in the village of Barewal Awana. He came from a Jat Sikh family and had served in the military, a detail that earned him deep respect among villagers. Few people, aside from the mailman Mr. Murari Lal, former classmates, or old coworkers, ever addressed him by name. Most simply called him "Baba," a title of reverence that suited both his age and his service.

Tall and lean, with a well-built frame that hadn't faded with time, Baba stood close to six feet. His beard had turned almost entirely white, and his slow but purposeful walk suggested he was well into his seventies. There was a quiet dignity in the way he carried himself, in the way he spoke, a presence that drew attention without ever asking for it.

Baba, a veteran of the Indian Army, had spent most of his life in military service. After retirement, he never worked for wages again, even though that meant living off a meager pension. Despite his long-standing service to the country, many in the village avoided him. They believed he carried an evil eye, a superstition that claimed misfortune would befall those who crossed his path or became the subject of his words.

But my father, Bahadur Singh, whom we affectionately called Bapu ji, was not one to be swayed by such beliefs. He had a radical way of thinking and firmly rejected the idea that a person could bring bad luck simply by existing. To him, the notion of an evil eye was just superstition, not something to shape one's treatment of another human being. Because of this, Baba was always welcome at our shop. Bapu ji treated him with consistent respect and hospitality.

Whenever Baba stopped by, we'd offer him a seat and ask what he'd like to eat or drink. In the summer, he asked for a glass of cold water; in winter, a cup of hot tea. He would linger at the shop for an hour or more, sometimes talking, sometimes simply sitting in quiet observation.

There was another reason Baba visited often. Some time ago, Bapu ji had borrowed money from him. Though the debt remained unpaid, all Baba ever got in return was Bapu ji's earnest promise that he would repay it, eventually, swearing by God as his witness. It was perhaps this mix of obligation and old-world trust that brought Baba back, again and again.

Occasionally, when Baba stopped by and didn't see Bapu ji at the shop, he would complain.

"Why is it that whenever I come to see him, he's either off shopping in the city or busy with something else? Are you sure he's not hiding in the back room?"

Even though many years had passed since Baba's retirement from the army, his manner of speaking and sense of discipline remained unchanged. He carried himself as though he were still serving. The way he used harsh language and nicknames, especially for those younger than him, reflected what he claimed was customary in the military. It also hinted that he may have held a high-ranking position during his service.

That same strictness, perhaps, explained why his family didn't seem to care for him much. He often complained about being neglected or ignored at home. Whenever he spoke of it, Bapu ji would nod along and take his side.

"The modern generation lacks traditional values," Bapu ji would say. "They'll understand only when they reach our age."

Whenever he said that, he would glance toward me, not sharply, but just enough to make it feel like his words were more for my benefit than for Baba's.

That same day, after we had received the telegram and the old women who had come to offer their sympathies had left, Baba stepped into our shop and took his usual seat. He ran his left hand slowly over his mustache and beard, his eyes fixed ahead rather than on Bapu ji. Then, in a voice that carried the usual weight of disappointment, he began,

"Bahadur Singh, tell me, what wrong did I do that my family treats me like this…"

But he didn't finish. His words trailed off the moment he noticed my father sitting unusually still, silent, his gaze fixed on the ground. Something in the air told Baba that things weren't as they normally were. Without skipping a beat, he shifted his tone and asked, more carefully this time, what was going on. What had made Bapu ji look so grim? When no response came from my father, Baba slowly turned to me instead. After taking the glass of cold water I had brought for him, Baba asked,

"Did the women say something to him that upset him?"

I told him the truth. I explained the telegram, and how the university scholarship required me to pay the full fee of Rupees 107.50, just over thirteen dollars, within the next two or three days. That, I said, was what had silenced my father. Baba looked at him for a moment, then said gently,

"Bahadur Singh, you are a man of faith. Don't worry. Just trust God. He will take care of it."

Without finishing the water or returning to the complaints he had started earlier about his own family, Baba stood and quietly stepped out of the shop. He walked off in the direction of the elementary school, which sat about half a mile away. Bapu ji didn't speak. He just looked at me with a tired, knowing expression, one that seemed to echo his words from earlier: As soon as you ask for money, people leave instantly.

An hour passed without a word spoken. Nothing changed at home. No one said anything. I saw Bapu ji seated quietly, flipping through the red-covered notebook where he kept track of customers who had bought groceries on credit and still hadn't paid. Nearby, my mother had opened her Gutka, softly reading verses of Gurbani. That was their usual response whenever we faced a serious financial worry, Bapu ji turning to his records, Ma turning to prayer.

I thought about stepping outside to join my friends, just to distract myself, but the moment I glanced at my father, I gave up on the idea. Instead, I lay down on the cot in the back room, my thoughts drifting toward the stories he'd told us, tales of his life before the partition, moments of hardship, pride, and generosity.

At some point, I must have fallen asleep. It wasn't until Ma gently shook me awake that I realized how much time had passed.

"The tea's ready," she said. "It's waiting for you."

After finishing my tea, unsure of what to do next, I stepped outside to see how the day was unfolding. People had started to move about, and I spotted a few of my neighborhood friends gathered near the shop. I joined them for a moment, just as I noticed the Baba walking back, this time at a brisk pace.

He looked unusually determined, almost hurried, as though he'd forgotten something important. My curiosity got the better of me, so I quietly followed him back into the shop.

Without glancing at Bapu ji, Baba said, "Look, Bahadur Singh, didn't I tell you? God always provides. Just like that, my pension came in today. I wasn't expecting it until a day or two later. But I happened to see Mr. Murari Lal walking back to school, and I asked if the pension had come in. He smiled and handed it over right then."

He held up the cash in his hand. "Here it is, Rupees 110. But this is only for Paul's fees. Not a paisa for anything else."

After receiving the money, Bapu ji handed it to me without hesitation, almost as if echoing Baba's intent. It was his silent way of agreeing, of acknowledging that this act was meant for me. He thanked Baba with quiet sincerity, calling it a "Godly gesture."

Just before leaving, Baba turned and added, "And don't forget to return the money within a month." Bapu ji responded with folded hands and a bowed forehead, a gesture of respect and commitment.

Once Baba had gone, Bapu ji looked at me and said, "For the world he may be a man with an evil eye, but for us, he has proven to be someone sent by God, a man with a merciful gaze."

With the money in my hand, I felt weightless. That night, I could barely sleep. The thought looped endlessly in my mind: I'm going to college. I'm really going. The feeling was overwhelming, a mix of disbelief and joy that refused to let me rest.

The following day, I made my way to the university and officially registered for my first trimester, eager to begin a new chapter, and to receive the first installment of my scholarship.

For those of us fresh out of high school, the bachelor's degree was a five-year journey. The length of the program didn't worry me as much as maintaining the scholarship, which was vital not only for my education but for the well-being of my family. Fortunately, my strength in mathematics and physics proved to be a lifeline. Those skills helped me retain the scholarship through the entire program.

But when I graduated, that privilege ended. With no scholarship to depend on, I began searching for a job, urgently, as it had become crucial for our family's survival. At the same time, as a precaution, I applied for admission into the M.Sc. program at the same university, hoping to secure another scholarship in case the job search didn't bear fruit. A few months later, still unemployed, I received confirmation of my admission into the master's program at PAU, this time with a substantial scholarship that felt like a new lease on life.

As for returning the money to Baba, I can't say exactly when I did, whether it was after finishing my bachelor's or during my master's. But I know without doubt that I returned it, most likely when my scholarship had significantly increased. By then, Baba had stopped visiting our shop, so I went to his home instead.

He was sitting quietly on a cot bed in his front yard, looking frail and worn. As I handed him the money, his face lit up, not because the money had finally come back to him, but because he was simply happy to see me. In all those years, he had never once asked for it.

My Love for Math & Physics

When it came to mathematics and physics, I had always stood out, even in my school days. It was rare for me to score anything less than a perfect 100% in either subject during exams. My teachers often expressed surprise at how quickly I could solve problems, even the ones designed to be tricky or unconventional.

One such moment stands out clearly in my memory. I was in 10th grade, and our class of nearly sixty students had grown loud and restless while waiting for the teacher. Just then, our school principal, clearly irritated by the noise, stormed in from his office. Hoping to quiet us down, he decided to distract us with a challenge.

He stood at the front of the class and said, "I am 56 years old today. Tell me, how old were you when I was your age?"

The room went silent. It was a clever question, clearly meant to engage our minds and regain control of the class, but it left most of my classmates puzzled and unsure.

Since most of us were around eighteen years old, answering the question meant calculating our age thirty-eight years ago, when the principal himself had been eighteen. That would place the timeline well before any of us were born. Realizing that, a complete hush fell over the room.

The principal scanned the room, noticing the absence of any raised hands. He repeated the question, this time louder, making sure everyone had heard him and had time to think it through.

Several minutes went by. Still, not a single hand went up, except one. Slowly, I raised mine. The principal's gaze landed on me, and he nodded, signaling me to answer.

"Minus twenty?" I replied, a bit unsure.

My reasoning was simple. If I was eighteen then, and thirty-eight years had passed since the principal had been my age, that would mean I hadn't even been born yet. I would have been twenty years from being born, hence, minus twenty.

The principal looked genuinely surprised when he heard my answer, and to my astonishment, he confirmed that it was correct. So surprised, in fact, that he spent the next thirty minutes lecturing the rest of the class about why they hadn't been able to figure it out. For the sake of clarity, he asked me to explain how I had come up with the answer.

I told him that only the day before, our physics teacher had explained how temperatures could fall below zero degrees Celsius. That concept had stuck with me. So when the principal posed his question, I imagined my birth year as the zero mark and simply applied that same logic in reverse.

It wasn't until I got to college, though, that I began to realize just how naturally gifted I was in math and physics. It wasn't only the professors who noticed, some of the top students in my class were equally intrigued. They'd often follow me after lectures, trying to understand how I could arrive at the correct answers so quickly. On occasion, they'd even treat me to a glass of hot milk at the campus canteen, knowing well that I didn't drink tea, just to get help with solving tough problems.

In one such incident, our well-respected math teacher, Mr. Saini, gave the class a quiz. It was his usual way of preparing us before moving on to the next chapter. There were around fifty students in the room, and he assured us we could take as much time as we needed to solve it.

As was often the case, he had barely finished writing the problem on the board when I stood up and called out my answer. Mr. Saini smiled knowingly and gestured for me to sit down. He didn't check the answer or challenge it. In previous classes, he had grown so used to my quick and accurate responses that he assumed correctness without question.

After a few minutes passed and no one else offered a solution, Mr. Saini told the class to treat the quiz as a home assignment and return with their answers the next day.

After class, a few of the top students asked if I could walk them through my solution. We went to the library and spent hours trying to retrace my steps, but strangely, I couldn't replicate the answer I had given in class. That's when it dawned on me: I had made a mistake.

The next day, I approached Mr. Saini and confessed the error. He looked surprised, even skeptical. He flipped through his notes, did the math himself, and finally nodded. "You're right," he said. "It's a small error, but I honestly didn't think you were capable of making one."

In another such instance, my knack for solving complex physics problems came sharply into focus. Our professor, increasingly frustrated by students repeatedly postponing the scheduled exam, often citing campus strikes or conflicts with other exams, decided to teach the entire class a lasting lesson.

He gave us an exceptionally difficult exam, deliberately crafted with little time to solve the questions. His intent was clear: to catch us unprepared and make us pay for our earlier evasions. And he succeeded. Out of nearly 250 students, more than 200 failed outright and were forced to re-enroll in the course. A few students managed to scrape by with a 'C' or a 'B'. But only one student earned an 'A'.

To my own disbelief, that student was me. Perhaps it was my genuine love for the subject or the way my mind naturally clicked with the logical challenges of physics. But whatever the reason, I stood alone with the top grade, surrounded by a campus buzzing with surprise. Even I struggled to accept the result at first. It felt surreal.

What most people didn't know was that my strength in Math and Physics wasn't just about talent, it was also a matter of survival. These two subjects alone were enough to lift my overall grade point average to the level needed to keep my scholarship, which I relied on heavily to continue my education.

Another hidden reason behind my performance was a habit I had carried with me since fifth grade, ever since the day I was punished for playing with marbles instead of doing my homework. From that point on, I made it a rule never to skip an assignment. Over the years, I strengthened this habit by adding another practice: I would always review the chapter my teacher planned to cover the next day, as outlined in the curriculum. This routine not only kept me prepared but also explained why I could often answer class quizzes so quickly.

I should add that I did well in many other subjects too. However, since those were more subjective and competitive in nature, it was Math and Physics that gave me a clear edge. They were consistent, quantifiable, and predictable, the kind of advantage that translated directly into a high GPA and, more importantly, the continuation of my scholarship.

My First Pair of Pants

This story wouldn't feel complete without providing the context that led to it. I'm talking about the events that occurred before I was even born, and what my parents had to endure. In 1947, when India was partitioned into two nations, millions of people were forced to leave everything behind. My parents were no exception. They had to leave behind everything they knew and loved in what became Pakistan, except for their seven children. They all boarded what was known as the 'death train,' making a perilous journey to the other side, India.

They were fortunate to have escaped the violence that claimed so many lives. At that time, they had no money, no place to live, no assets to sell, and no skills or education to help them find work. Their only sense of security was their survival, and they were deeply thankful to God for that. Yet life for them, and for the family, was filled with hardship and struggle.

After about a year of moving from one shelter to the next, they finally found a small place to call home. This modest dwelling was located in Kucha (Street) #9 in the Field Gunj area of Ludhiana city, where I would be born in 1950. But soon after settling in, municipal authorities ordered us to vacate.

A man known to my father offered us temporary accommodation in the village of Kokri Kalan, in what was then Ferozepur district. With no other option, we moved there. It was in Kokri Kalan that my younger brother was born in 1954, bringing the total number of siblings to nine, eight brothers and one sister. Three years later, our family moved back to Ludhiana for a couple of years before relocating once more, this time to Sri Ganganagar, Rajasthan. Throughout their lives, my parents continued moving from place to place until, in 1968, they finally settled in Barewal Awana, a village on the outskirts of Ludhiana district.

A villager who owned several acres of farmland generously offered us a small house to live in for a modest rent of 12 rupees per month, about one and a half US dollars at the time. The house had a single large room, roughly 20 by 15 feet, with a small veranda outside, about 20 by 8 feet in size.

My father, whom we affectionately called Bapu ji, partitioned a section of the main room to use for business. With a bit of help from a local lender, he borrowed enough money to open a small grocery store. Most of the inventory he stocked was obtained on credit, which meant the wholesale prices he paid were slightly higher than what other village shopkeepers paid in cash. As a result, he was at a competitive disadvantage from the beginning.

This situation left my father with only two options: either raise his prices above those of his competitors or significantly reduce his profit margins just to keep the store running. In practice, he chose the latter. As a result, most of his customers were low-wage brick-kiln workers who had migrated from neighboring states and often bought goods on credit, sometimes settling their accounts monthly, but often not at all. Many of these laborers would abruptly leave the area or return home without notice, and with them went the money they owed.

There was little to no steady income. We survived largely on borrowed essentials, food, clothing, and even goodwill. For months at a time, we were unable to pay even the modest rent. Bapu ji, once a man of wealth and stature before the partition, had grown accustomed to seeking help, never begging on the streets, but humbly approaching those who had once known him, hoping for kindness in return.

That habit of frequently seeking help gradually alienated many villagers and former acquaintances. Some, wary of being asked for money again, began to avoid the store altogether. But not everyone turned away. There were those who, for reasons known only to the villagers, were disliked or marginalized by their own families or community. These individuals found in Bapu ji a kind and attentive listener. They would visit him often, linger for hours, and share their frustrations freely.

While their presence didn't exactly help the business. In fact, it sometimes discouraged genuine customers, Bapu ji didn't seem to mind. These visitors occasionally loaned him small amounts of money or even helped run the store, which allowed him to pay off lingering debts or cover essentials like rent. So, whatever damage their presence caused to the store's reputation was of little concern to him. In truth, the shop had become less of a business venture and more of a lifeline, a reason to stay connected to others, and a subtle way to continue asking for support without directly begging.

Despite the unrelenting hardship, Bapu ji somehow always managed to keep food on the table and a roof over our heads. How he did it was often a mystery to us. He never gave a clear picture of how much money he owed or to whom, perhaps because he had long since lost track himself. The number of lenders had grown so large that the names and amounts blurred together in his mind.

Over time, it became common for people to refuse him further help. But if this frustrated Bapu ji, he never showed it. He seemed to have developed a sort of emotional armor against rejection. When someone did come forward to help, it was more than a relief, it was an event worth celebrating. He would speak of that person with admiration, retelling the story proudly and often, holding them up as a rare example of generosity.

One such person was Baba Kala Singh, an old man with a reputation for having an "evil eye," who had recently stunned everyone by giving Bapu ji his entire pension just so I could pay my tuition fees.

But this time, it wasn't just Bapu ji who was filled with joy and gratitude toward Baba Kala Singh, I was equally elated. Without Baba's timely help, I wouldn't have been able to fulfill my dream of attending college, a dream tied not just to personal ambition but to the survival of our family. The scholarship I aimed for was not simply a mark of academic success; it was a financial lifeline.

Higher education had become more than just an aspiration, it was etched deeply into my mind as the only escape from poverty. Back then, college was seen as the singular path to upward mobility, and I had set my heart on it early. A major influence behind this mindset was the work of Nanak Singh, the renowned Punjabi novelist. I devoured his novels during my high school and college years, borrowing them freely from the local library. His stories, steeped in hope, resilience, and human dignity, shaped not only my worldview but my belief in the transformative power of education.

The novels laid bare the vicious cycle that people born into poverty were forced to endure, especially within the rigid confines of the Indian social system. They impressed upon me the idea that higher education was not just an opportunity, but the most reliable path out of that cycle. What I didn't realize at the time, though, was that gaining admission into college was only the beginning. There were many hidden expenses: transportation, textbooks, stationery, lunch, clothing, shoes, even the cost of trying to socialize with peers and participate in student life.

But having grown up watching my parents navigate hardship, I made a quiet decision, I would not burden them any further. By then, I had absorbed enough from their resilience to know how to ask for help when needed, to stretch what little I had, and to get by through resourcefulness and, at times, sheer will.

Attending college in pajamas and slippers, while most other boys came dressed in crisp bell-bottom pants and polished shoes, no longer embarrassed me. I had grown used to being different. I also made it a point to politely decline free offers from classmates or staff, whether it was for a tea outing, a movie, or a party, because I didn't want to feel obliged to return the favor someday.

Whenever possible, I picked up part-time work or tutored younger children in the village, scraping together whatever extra money I could. Still, I knew that the real key to sustaining both my education and my family's survival lay in one thing: maintaining my scholarship. That meant achieving top grades and collecting academic awards, no matter how uncomfortable I felt attending the ceremonies where they were handed out. With my outdated clothes and worn shoes, I preferred to avoid such public occasions unless the college administration insisted I attend.

Wearing pajamas and slippers to college became my daily norm. I was likely the only student dressed that way, and soon, my attire became something of a trademark, my unofficial identity during the first two years of college. But everything began to shift in my third year, when my academic achievements placed me on the Dean's List.

Suddenly, I was invited to attend meetings with the Dean alongside other top-performing students. These gatherings, though meant to be honors, started to stir something new in me: a sense of discomfort. I began to feel self-conscious showing up in my usual clothes, especially when everyone else looked sharp in their pressed western outfits.

At one particular meeting, the Dean pulled me aside. He informed me that a prominent politician would soon be visiting the campus to preside over an awards ceremony. With a warm but firm tone, he said he expected students, especially me, to attend the event dressed appropriately.

Then, with a kindness I hadn't anticipated, he offered to help if I needed anything to make that happen.

That conversation with the Dean weighed on my mind more than I expected. When I got home that evening, I found my elder sister had arrived earlier that day to stay with us for a week. She immediately sensed something was off and asked me what was bothering me.

I told her everything, about the upcoming awards ceremony, the Dean's request, and my growing discomfort with showing up in pajamas when everyone else would be dressed in proper western clothes. I explained that borrowing a shirt wasn't the issue, but getting a pair of pants was a different story. That was the part giving me a headache.

Her response caught me off guard. Tears welled up in her eyes as she said that if I could manage to buy a piece of fabric and have it professionally cut, she would be happy to sew the pants for me. She even offered to extend her stay so she could help me learn the sewing myself and finish the job if needed. Her resolve stirred something deep in me, and I accepted her offer without hesitation.

The next day, I took Bapu ji to a fabric shop in the city, one where the owner knew him well. Leaning on Bapu ji's goodwill, I was able to buy the cloth on credit, a piece just large enough to make a single pair of pants.

Then came the question of who would cut the fabric. Fortunately, the answer was closer than I expected. Our landlord's daughter, who lived next door in the village, had recently completed training in tailoring, though only for women's garments. When I asked if she could cut the fabric for my pants, she initially refused, saying it was beyond her expertise.

But I persisted, assuring her that I wouldn't hold her accountable if things went wrong. Reluctantly, she agreed. Not only that, she even offered to let me borrow her sewing machine if my sister was going to teach me how to use it. I gave her my pajamas for measurements.

Over the next week, each evening became a lesson. My sister would sit beside me, guiding my hands as I struggled with the machine, trying to follow her instructions. I had never sewn before, and the learning curve was steep. Mistakes were constant. Threads would tangle, seams had to be undone and redone.

The side pockets, in particular, drove me to frustration, they took forever to attach properly. But I kept at it, reworking every flawed stitch until it began to take shape. And then, just over a week later, my very first pair of pants was complete. They fit. They looked real. I was thrilled beyond words.

I felt as if I had conquered Mount Everest. The next day, wearing those pants to college, I became an instant attraction. My friends and classmates quickly noticed and came over to congratulate me, some with warm handshakes and playful grins. Even students I barely knew approached with half-smiles, said hello, and moved on, leaving me slightly confused and, admittedly, a bit uncomfortable.

For some, I realized, my change of wardrobe meant more than just a new look. I had been a kind of unspoken benchmark, the student who walked around in pajamas while everyone else dressed up. My presence had allowed others to feel a little better about themselves, even if silently. Now, that comforting contrast had vanished.

The award ceremony came and went. Mr. Zail Singh, then the Home Minister of India and future President, graced the event, handing out awards and degrees to students. Like everyone else, I received mine and had a photograph taken with him. Over the years, I would collect other photos from ceremonies like this one. But of all those pictures, only one stayed with me, the one where I was wearing the pants I had stitched with my own hands.

It wasn't the presence of a high-ranking politician that made the moment unforgettable. It was the quiet triumph sewn into every seam of that pair of pants. That photo, more than any award, reminded me of what I had overcome.

Receiving an award for academic excellence from Mr. Zail Singh, then the Home Minister of India

Fighting with Appendicitis and Chicken Pox

In early 1975, while preparing for the final year of my two-year M.Sc. degree program at Punjab Agricultural University (PAU), I was suddenly struck by appendicitis. Caused commonly by Escherichia coli bacteria, appendicitis is an inflammation of the appendix, a small, finger-like pouch projecting from the colon on the lower right side of the abdomen. The condition brings with it a sharp, often unbearable abdominal pain and typically requires urgent surgery to remove the infected organ.

As the infection worsened, the pain became intense, leaving me restless and unable to concentrate. On the advice of my classmates, I rushed to the university's health clinic, a modest facility on campus with a physician available for students and staff, offering basic treatment and first aid.

After a brief examination, the doctor confirmed what I had feared: I had appendicitis and required immediate surgery. He informed me that an ambulance had already been arranged to take me to a nearby hospital. Before I could even fully process the diagnosis, he added another layer of anxiety, I would likely need to pay a significant sum upon admission, possibly far more than my scholarship allowance could ever cover. The university, he explained, would not be able to cover any off-campus medical expenses, and I had no health insurance or savings.

As the ambulance sped toward the hospital, I asked the driver to make a quick stop at my elder brother's house, hoping to borrow some money. He agreed. But when we arrived, my brother was not home. His wife, my sister-in-law, answered the door. With a regretful expression, she said she couldn't help. The ambulance decided to not wait any longer or go see someone else but drive straight to the hospital.

As the ambulance made its way toward the hospital, my thoughts shifted from physical pain to a growing anxiety about my academic future. What if I couldn't take my upcoming exams? The possibility of delaying my degree completion weighed heavily on me. Worse yet, failing to appear could put my scholarship at risk, something my entire family had come to depend on. The urgency of that fear momentarily dulled the pain of appendicitis, at least in my mind.

Just then, the driver announced our arrival at Christian Medical College (CMC) Hospital. He pulled up near the waiting room and helped me out. A hospital staff member stepped in and guided me inside. By this point, the pain had become unbearable. I could do little more than lie on the floor, motionless, trying not to cry out.

The staff informed me that admission required immediate cash payment. There were no exceptions. With no money in my pocket and no guarantee of help arriving anytime soon, all I could do was wait, and pray. I prayed not only for relief but for some unexpected mercy to step in and change my fate.

Apparently, my prayer was answered. My elder brother, whom I had just missed at his house earlier, finally arrived at the hospital with enough cash in hand. Breathless and repeatedly apologizing for not being home when I came by, he wasted no time in getting me admitted as an emergency case.

Fortunately, I didn't have to wait long for the surgery. Later, the surgeon would tell me I was lucky to have made it in time. Any further delay could have resulted in a ruptured appendix, which would have greatly complicated the procedure. The operation went well, but it required me to remain hospitalized for nearly three weeks to fully recover.

Those three weeks were oddly transformative. My physical pain gradually subsided, replaced by a sense of calm and introspection. I also had the chance to meet a range of fellow patients, each with their own struggles and stories. Among them was a Sadhu, a holy man, who had come in for a similar operation. His quiet presence and spiritual demeanor made a lasting impression on me, offering unexpected comfort during my healing.

The Sadhu's condition was far more severe than mine. His appendix had already ruptured, forcing the doctors to open his entire abdominal area to clean out the infection. After his surgery, he was moved to the bed right next to mine in a large open ward that held twenty to thirty other patients recovering from various procedures.

Having him as a neighbor was both a blessing and, at times, a challenge. We quickly became friends, and our conversations helped the long days pass more easily. He spoke openly about his life as a Sadhu, his travels, his preaching, and even the secrets behind some of the magic tricks he used to captivate people. There was something disarming in his honesty, and though I was initially skeptical, I found myself fascinated by his stories. His presence brought a strange mix of mysticism and humanity to the otherwise clinical setting of the ward.

The not-so-good part of having the Sadhu as a neighbor was the steady stream of visitors who came to see him. His many followers visited throughout the day, often speaking loudly, sometimes weeping at the sight of his fragile state. Their constant presence made it difficult for me to rest, and at times, the noise became overwhelming.

On the brighter side, his visitors never came empty-handed. They brought baskets of food, fresh fruit, boiled eggs, and homemade parathas stuffed with mashed potatoes or chopped fenugreek leaves. The Sadhu, still recovering and unable to eat solid food, would turn to me after his guests left and say, "Eat what you like, and share the rest." He meant it every time. I had never seen so much food in one place, let alone had the chance to enjoy it. For a student living on a tight budget, it was a feast, and a rare one at that. It truly was one of the best times I can remember during my hospital stay. But like many good things, it didn't come without consequences.

As soon as I was discharged from the hospital, I came down with chicken pox. I couldn't help but suspect the boiled eggs the Sadhu had generously insisted I eat, perhaps some weren't fully cooked. I had no way of proving it, of course, but I had read that eggs could sometimes carry the virus. Still, it wasn't the illness itself that worried me most, it was the looming threat of losing my scholarship if I didn't perform well in the final exams. This was my last year in the master's program, and with the classes I'd already missed due to the appendicitis surgery, I could hardly afford any more setbacks.

The timing couldn't have been worse. The university had a strict policy: no student with an infectious disease was allowed to attend class. So even after I began feeling a little better, I wasn't allowed into the classroom until I had fully recovered. The virus hit me hard, not just physically, but mentally, with the anxiety it caused.

Thankfully, my friends came through for me. They would meet me in an open courtyard, reading their notes aloud from a distance so I could listen without risking anyone's health. They also borrowed textbooks from the library on my behalf. With their support and the study materials, I managed to catch up quickly. By the time exams rolled around, it felt like I had never fallen behind. I passed with ease, retained my scholarship, and completed my degree right on schedule.

With my master's degree completed, I turned my attention once again to finding a suitable job. I applied to several openings that matched my area of expertise, each time submitting my credentials with optimism. But the results were disappointingly familiar. Just like before, there were no offers. Most employers didn't even acknowledge receipt of my application, let alone provide any feedback about why I wasn't selected. Despite my strong academic record, I seemed to hit the same invisible wall, a quiet but persistent barrier that blocked progress without explanation.

However, this time, I had learned from the past. I didn't let the silence or rejection slow me down. Instead of waiting endlessly for a job offer that might never come, I immediately applied to the Ph.D. program at PAU, confident that my academic performance would secure me a spot. It did. My grades were still among the highest, and I was not only accepted into the doctoral program but awarded an even more generous scholarship than before. It was a validation of my resilience and a reminder that sometimes, forging your own path forward is the best kind of success.

Ah, My New Bike!

Established in 1962 through collaboration with Ohio State University in the United States, Punjab Agricultural University quickly emerged as one of India's premier institutions for agricultural education and research. It attracted top-tier students from across the country and abroad, earning a reputation for academic excellence and innovation. Notably, the University played a pivotal role in initiating the Green Revolution, a movement that transformed India into a self-sufficient nation in food production.

Spread across hundreds of acres, PAU was more than just a place of learning, it was a thriving campus community. The University had constructed extensive residential facilities, offering on-campus housing for a nominal fee to students and staff alike. As a result, more than 90 percent of enrolled students, along with a significant portion of the faculty and staff, lived on campus. This residential setting fostered a strong sense of community and allowed for vibrant academic and social interaction within the University grounds.

Living on campus undeniably provided a peaceful, focused environment and saved precious time for students. However, not everyone could afford that privilege. Among the roughly 10 percent of students who lived off-campus were those like me, who couldn't bear the costs of the comparatively luxurious on-campus lifestyle. We either rented modest rooms nearby or stayed with family, commuting daily using whatever means were available. In my case, I lived about five kilometers from the university and had to make that trip every day.

A bicycle quickly proved to be the most affordable, efficient, and practical way not only to commute but also to get around the vast campus with its widely spread academic buildings and experimental fields. In the past, I had always managed to borrow an old bicycle from someone kind enough to lend it, usually one in disrepair. I often had to stop mid-ride to fix a loose chain or adjust a tire, sometimes more than once during a single commute.

The real trouble came from my clothing. Whether I was wearing a pajama or later switched to pants, the bottom of my right leg would frequently get caught in the greasy chain. Each time, I'd have to dismount, untangle the fabric, and try to wipe off the smudges, never entirely successful. The thought of buying a new bicycle often crossed my mind, mostly in hopes of sparing my clothes from constant damage and embarrassment. But the thought was always short-lived. Financial hardship had the final say.

In 1976, when I entered the Ph.D. program at PAU, my scholarship saw a significant increase, from 400 to 600 Indian rupees per month. On top of that, I was earning extra income by tutoring village kids. With all this newfound financial stability, I figured I could finally afford a new bike. I headed to a bike shop in Ludhiana, the city known for producing India's most popular bicycles. The salesman recommended an Atlas brand bike, assuring me it was a good choice. He also persuaded me to purchase insurance, warning me that thefts of new bikes were common in the area. I followed his advice.

The next morning, as I rode the new bike to campus, I couldn't help but feel as though I was riding a Mercedes-Benz.

As I rode my new bicycle toward campus, I found myself scanning the faces of passersby, curious to see if anyone noticed. I wasn't sure why I expected a reaction, but it felt like the moment deserved some recognition. To my surprise, no one paid any attention. No admiring glances, no comments, just another person on a bike.

But as soon as I entered the university grounds, the response changed dramatically. It reminded me of the time I wore my first pair of custom-tailored pants a few years earlier, how people noticed every detail. On campus, students and friends were quick to comment on the bicycle's brand, make, model, and even its finer features. Some joked that I should throw a party to celebrate the purchase. I laughed it off and chose not to entertain the idea.

A few months passed, and I had grown deeply attached to my new bicycle. It was more than just a means of transport, it had become a source of pride and relief. Gone were the days of struggling with loose chains or stopping mid-commute to wipe black grease off my pants in full view of others. The bike saved me time, spared me embarrassment, and gave me a sense of ease that I hadn't experienced before.

I always made a point to park it properly, using the officially designated stands and positioning it carefully so that others wouldn't accidentally damage it. The university campus, with its strong sense of community and visible security presence, was generally considered safe from theft. Because of that, no one really bothered with using locking chains or belts to secure their bikes, including me.

But then the inevitable happened, the bike was stolen. I believe the person who took it must have been watching me for some time, noticing how I'd often spend hours inside the library, completely immersed in my research projects. That probably made it easier for them to strike.

I was devastated. A sinking feeling set in, and I wasn't sure what to do next. The thought of having to ask someone once again to lend me a used bicycle filled me with embarrassment.

Still, I found some comfort in remembering that I had purchased insurance. Surely, I thought, I would be compensated, either with a refund or a replacement. That hope lifted my spirits a bit. But when I contacted the insurance company, they informed me that I would need to file a First Information Report (FIR) with the local police and submit a copy to them before they could process the claim. It sounded simple enough, and I was hopeful that everything would be resolved soon.

The next morning, armed with all the necessary documents, receipt of purchase, insurance papers, and a written statement, I went to the nearby police station to file a report. I explained the situation to the officer on duty and requested a First Information Report, as required by the insurance company.

He listened half-heartedly, then casually informed me that the officer authorized to issue such reports was out on assignment and that I should come back another time. When I asked for a specific day or time, he simply shrugged and said, "I wish I could tell you that," before walking away with a murky smile that made me uneasy.

Undeterred, I returned the next day, but the response was the same, another vague excuse, another brush-off. This routine repeated for over a week. Each visit ended in disappointment, and every day brought a new excuse. Eventually, a few of my close friends pulled me aside and gently hinted that perhaps the officers were waiting for me to offer a bribe before moving forward. The very thought made me uncomfortable. My conscience resisted the idea. I wasn't ready to bend that way. So, I continued waiting, hoping that honesty and persistence would pay off.

On my final visit to the police station, frustrated and disheartened, I began walking back when I ran into someone familiar, Mr. Gill, my old neighbor from the village. He was seated outside his office, a modest setup for his trucking company, Gill Transport. The moment he spotted me, he called out warmly, waving for me to join him.

I took a seat beside him, grateful for a break. Though he was much older, Mr. Gill had always shown me respect, perhaps because I had once tutored his son back in the village. Studying my face, he asked, "What's wrong? You look like something's weighing heavy on you."

I opened up and shared the full story: the stolen bicycle, the insurance claim, and the endless runaround I'd been getting from the police in trying to get a simple loss report.

Now, in our village, there was a common perception, spoken quietly but often, that transport business owners like Mr. Gill were entangled in more than just logistics. Many believed they had ties to the drug trade and maintained their operations by keeping the right officials well-fed and well-connected. Mr. Gill, with his frequent visits from police officers and local bigwigs, fit that image for many. While I didn't fully buy into those whispers, I couldn't ignore how often I saw law enforcement hanging around his office with unusual familiarity.

So, as I told my story, part of me felt like I was venting to someone with insider authority, as if he could make the system move. I wasn't wrong. Mr. Gill listened in silence, his expression darkening with each word. Without responding directly, he reached for his phone and dialed the police station I had just left.

As I walked away from Mr. Gill's office and back toward the university campus, a heavy wave of reflection came over me. I couldn't help but think, what a broken, upside-down system we live in. Here I was, a Ph.D. student, trying to follow the rules, seeking nothing more than a simple report for an insurance claim, and no one cared. But a man like Mr. Gill, who hadn't even finished high school, who had twice been arrested and imprisoned on drug trafficking charges, had every door open to him. People rushed to help him, even if it meant bending rules or breaking laws. It was disheartening. A real shame.

And yet, in that moment, a quiet pride stirred in me. I hadn't given in. I hadn't bribed anyone or compromised my values. I had stayed the course, however frustrating. My thoughts drifted to Bapu ji, my father, an honest man who, despite hardship and limited means, had always taught us that real success came from honesty and hard work. He used to say, "If you want a name that lasts, do right by your conscience."

At the time, neither he nor I could have imagined how far those values would carry me. Years later, raised on those lessons, I would find myself traveling across continents, negotiating with officials from foreign governments, and speaking at international conferences as a representative of no less than the most powerful nation in the world, the United States of America.

That old two-wheeled bicycle, once my proudest possession, had long been replaced by many-wheeled transport systems ferrying me around the globe. In 2007, I walked into the halls of Washington, D.C., to receive my second award from the Secretary of the U.S. Department of Agriculture, a historic moment for the Department, the first such recognition having come in 1996.

And standing there, I could feel it clearly: every success I had ever earned traced back to the integrity Bapu ji had instilled in me. His words had not only lasted, they had built my foundation.

Chapter III – Canada, Here I Come

How did I make to Canada?

S oon after completing my master's degree, and before formally entering the Ph.D. program at PAU Ludhiana in 1976, I began searching for a job that matched my qualifications and would provide a decent living. Several vacancies were advertised in newspapers and on notice boards, most requiring an M.Sc. as the minimum qualification. I applied to every position I believed was a good fit.

Despite my excellent academic record and grades, I didn't receive a single positive response. The most I heard was that my application would be kept on file in case the selected candidate declined or another opening arose. I was disappointed, but more so, I was puzzled. Many of the roles were filled either by those holding Ph.D. degrees or by individuals who lacked even the basic qualifications but had prior connections with the selection officials.

Once again, I found myself facing the realities of survival. I needed money, not just to live, but even to continue applying for jobs. So, I pivoted. Getting into a Ph.D. program made the most sense. It came with a reasonable scholarship and helped me avoid a gap in my resume while I figured out my next steps.

Fortunately, many staff members at PAU knew me well and respected my academic standing. Gaining admission into the program was straightforward. Since my M.Sc. thesis had been in Plant Virology, I chose to continue in the same field for my Ph.D. dissertation. I also believed it was a growing area with strong research potential and long-term impact.

Halfway through my first year in the Ph.D. program, a friend, one of my former classmates from the master's program at PAU, approached me with a handful of forms. He explained that they were for a Government of India scholarship, which offered just thirty slots nationwide for students to pursue higher studies abroad. The scholarships spanned across diverse fields, science, art, architecture, medicine, agriculture, even music.

He admitted he didn't meet the minimum qualifications himself but thought I might. "Take a look," he said. "If you're not interested, just toss them. I'm done with them anyway."

I chuckled and held the papers up. "Only thirty scholarships for the whole country? And you know how much connections matter in these decisions. What chance do you think I have?"

Still, the forms were already in my hands, and curiosity got the better of me. Instead of tossing them in the trash, I decided to toss them into a mailbox. Why not?

About a month later, I received a letter. To my surprise, I had cleared the initial round and was invited for an interview in

New Delhi. The letter outlined the interview date and explained how I could claim reimbursement for travel expenses. At first, I thought the interview might just be a formality, a token gesture by the government to appear impartial. But since they were paying for the trip either way, I figured I might as well enjoy the experience. I had never been to Delhi, and if nothing else, this would be my chance.

If for nothing else, I would at least get to visit the capital of India, Delhi, for the first time. So, more out of curiosity and for the experience, I took the train to Delhi and appeared for the interview.

About three months later, a letter arrived from the Government of India (GOI). As I opened it, I found a couple of pages that looked like they had been copied and recopied from an original typed using a stencil machine. Some lines were so faded they were nearly illegible. The language was vague, and apart from my name typed on the envelope, there was no personal mention anywhere in the document. In short, the letter congratulated me in general terms as one of the selected individuals, outlined the terms I needed to accept, and described the process that both the GOI and I would follow separately to secure admission to a foreign college or university for higher studies, in my case, a Ph.D. program in my chosen field.

I immediately assumed it was a clerical mistake. Surely, someone had typed my name on the envelope in error, and the letter wasn't meant for me. I filed it away and forgot about it.

Just a couple of months later, another letter arrived, this time addressed to me both on the envelope and inside the document. It contained a progress report from the GOI and asked me to provide a similar update on my side. It also urged me to begin gathering important travel-related documents like a passport, visa, and permission for currency exchange.

That's when I realized the selection was real. It wasn't a prank or a mix-up. My excitement shot through the roof.

At first, no one at home believed me when I told them. Even at the university, there was skepticism. As far as anyone knew, no one from PAU, or anyone with an agricultural background, for that matter, had ever been selected for that scholarship. Some even asked bluntly whether I had any connections in the government or if I'd paid someone under the table. But those who knew my story, someone who couldn't even afford proper pants in the first two years of college, someone who had once refused to bribe a police officer just to get a stolen bike report, believed me.

My Ph.D. advisor at PAU, Dr. Khatri, who had previously guided me through parts of the process, believed me wholeheartedly. He was overjoyed by the news and urged me not to let the opportunity pass.

On my way home from the University, my thoughts drifted to the many relatives, family friends, and members of our larger community, my brothers, nephews, uncles, who had tried for years to secure a visa to countries like the United States or Canada. They had visited consular offices in New

Delhi multiple times, only to be met with disappointment. And here I was, with everything seemingly falling into place without much effort or cost on my part. It felt surreal.

I had never seen myself as especially smart, at least not in the way that turned heads socially. I didn't keep up with movies or memorize clever dialogues. While other guys on campus spent their evenings flirting or taking slow walks toward the girls' hostel, I stayed back to play indoor games, table tennis, carom, chess, anything that kept me from such gatherings. My financial situation certainly kept me from socializing, but there was more to it. I had grown up in an environment where talk of girls, movies, and anything related to sex was taboo. That background shaped me into what I was: quiet, simple, a bit of a bookworm.

So being selected for the scholarship, despite all that, surprised me. It also made me feel proud. For once, I felt I had something solid to show for all the years I had remained in the background. I imagined being able to change my parents' lives, lifting the debt they had carried for decades, giving them the chance to enjoy the peace and dignity they had been denied since leaving Pakistan nearly thirty years ago. Maybe, God willing, I could eventually settle in the country where I would pursue my studies and bring them to live with me there. But a shadow lingered. Would my parents be willing to let me go in the meantime? I didn't know the answer, and that worried me. Just then, I realized I had reached home. My daydream ended abruptly.

I regretted having procrastinated those past few months, delaying applications to foreign universities and putting off gathering the travel documents I needed. But now I was in motion. Both the Government of India and I pushed forward. Almost simultaneously, we secured two offers: one from the University of Manitoba (U of M) in Winnipeg, Canada, and one from Imperial College in London. The GOI had favored the latter, but when I explained my preference for U of M, they honored my choice. Within two months, I was ready to depart for Canada.

My parents had mixed emotions. Though they were proud, they knew I would be gone for over four years. Still, they understood what this meant. In August 1977, the day of my departure arrived. An hour before I was to leave, our house filled with relatives, neighbors, and friends. Some came with garlands of flowers; others fed me ladoos with their eyes shining with pride and sadness. My mother kept wiping her tears, while my father stood silently nearby, lost in thought. Then the van, my brother had arranged it for the round trip, pulled up in front of our house. I turned to my younger brother and whispered for him to take care of our parents. With that, I stepped into the vehicle. Four family members, two brothers and two nephews came along to see me off. The airport was more than 200 miles away, a drive of six to seven hours. As we pulled away from home, the driver addressed us:

"We'll stop near Ambala for about twenty or thirty minutes to get petrol. If anyone wants to eat, drink, or use the washroom, that will be the time. If you need to stop elsewhere, just let me know." He added, "If traffic cooperates, we should be at the airport by 8 pm."

The driver seemed experienced in airport runs, familiar with the route and the typical concerns of travelers. His tone was informative but also practical, a subtle reminder that we would be responsible for all costs incurred along the way.

My flight was scheduled for around 2 a.m. the following morning, so arriving at the airport five to six hours ahead of time gave me a sense of comfort and control. In those days, given the road conditions, detours, unpredictable Delhi traffic, and the ever-looming risk of accidents or car trouble, it was normal to plan for a two-to-three-hour buffer. True to his word, the driver brought us to the airport right around 8 p.m.

For most of the ride, we sat in silence. The atmosphere in the van was heavy, not with words, but with everything that went unspoken.

When we finally pulled up near the departure terminal, the driver, eyeing the restriction signs and the stream of other vehicles, reminded us he couldn't stop for long. My younger brother spotted an unattended cart and quickly transferred my luggage onto it. The rest of the family moved toward me, one by one, arms open. The hugs came quietly but carried weight. My teenage nephews, unable to hold back, began to cry. I felt my throat tighten. My elder brother, ever composed, offered a final word, "OK, we need to get back into the van. Let us know when you reach safely, with full details."

I could only nod, my voice caught somewhere behind my eyes. Then, just like that, they were gone. I stood alone at the gate, watching the van disappear into the blur of tail lights and city sounds.

A few hours later, I was seated aboard a massive, double-decker 747 operated by Air India, heading toward Toronto. I had arranged to spend a week there with a long-time friend before continuing to my final destination, Winnipeg, Manitoba.

As the plane lifted through the thick monsoon clouds, I looked out at the city slowly fading beneath me. The weight of humidity gave way to cool, pressurized air inside the cabin, but my thoughts stayed rooted. I wasn't just leaving behind weather or geography. I was leaving behind a lifetime—my parents, my childhood friends, decades of financial struggle, and a version of myself that never thought this kind of escape was possible.

Somewhere between Delhi and Toronto, weariness overtook me. The days of preparations, the long drive, the airport chaos, all of it had drained me. After fastening my seatbelt and settling in, I barely remembered the plane's ascent. Sleep arrived like a gentle rescue, and I gave in without resistance.

My First Ever Flight in a Massive Plane

With two large suitcases stacked on a cart and a folder in hand holding my passport, air ticket, and admission papers from the University of Manitoba, I stepped through the terminal door marked for departing passengers. A slow-moving crowd filed in with me, each person carefully watched by a security guard who checked our documents one by one. Once cleared, I was directed by another uniformed official to a currency exchange window, where I converted a limited amount of Indian rupees into Canadian dollars, about six dollars, the maximum allowed under the Reserve Bank of India regulations at the time.

Inside the terminal, I was met with a festival-like atmosphere. Lights were bright, the space was buzzing, and luggage was scattered in every direction. Despite the general rush, most people were orderly and polite. Like me, many were first-time flyers, noticeably unsure, glancing around with uncertainty or following the better-informed travelers who seemed to know the way. I decided to shadow a fellow passenger who, like me, was headed to Toronto on the same Air India flight.

We waited in one line after another: first for the airline counter to check in our luggage and collect boarding passes, then at immigration for passport stamping, and finally through security checks to ensure we carried only approved items. These steps took nearly an hour before another staff member guided us toward our departure gate. As we walked, we passed others, some seated on chairs or even the floor, waiting for their turn to board. Some stood in lines for food, others for the restroom. It was a sea of activity.

With my suitcases checked in, I carried only my folder, which made it easier to navigate the crowd. As a solo traveler, I was lucky to spot an empty seat near my gate. I settled in and waited.

Eventually, airline staff appeared at the gate, signaling that boarding was about to begin. After a final pass through a quick-moving security check, I stepped into the aircraft. The flight crew greeted us warmly and directed us to our seats.

I was stunned the moment I entered the Boeing 747. I had read about its massive size, but seeing it in person was something else. It felt like a whole village had come together inside this flying marvel. There were two levels, and the seating seemed endless. I was seated in economy class, where rows were arranged ten seats across, with separate sections for kitchens, restrooms, and supply storage. Overhead compartments brimmed with carry-on bags and small suitcases.

Though I didn't get to see the upper deck, I imagined it was just as impressive. I found my seat and started fumbling with the seatbelt until a flight attendant noticed and kindly helped me buckle up. The seat next to mine was empty, a small relief on such a long journey. I quickly placed my folder there to claim the space. I'd picked up this tip from the same traveler I'd followed through the terminal, who had hoped to find an empty seat beside him to stretch out during the flight.

I scanned the rows, hoping to spot him again and see if he'd been as lucky. But he was nowhere to be found, perhaps seated in another section or already fast asleep.

The plane began to move slowly, making a few turns before stopping beside the runway, waiting for clearance. Soon enough, the pilot's voice came through the intercom, announcing that we had been cleared for takeoff and asking the crew to take their seats. The cabin lights dimmed. In minutes, we had lifted off, rising through thick monsoon clouds until we reached a cruising altitude of 33,000 feet.

Once in the air, everything became incredibly smooth, so still it felt like we weren't moving at all. The seatbelt signs turned off, and for a moment, it felt like I was floating in some quiet version of heaven. The pilot's voice returned, this time with good news: much better weather awaited us at our destination.

As the cabin settled into calm, I leaned back, thoughts drifting toward what I had recently read about Canada in magazines borrowed from the library. I hadn't slept in over 24 hours before boarding, so it didn't take long before sleep overtook me. Pretty soon, I was lost in dreams, one after another, until I was stirred by a soft voice.

"Excuse me."

I opened my eyes. The cabin was bright again, and a flight attendant stood beside me, holding a small, neatly folded white cloth with a pair of tongs.

"Would you like to have one?" she asked, her tone brisk, like someone trying to finish a list of tasks.

Still half-asleep and unsure what it was for, I nodded and accepted it. The cloth was warm and damp, as if it had just come out of a steamer. I looked around and noticed that other passengers were using theirs to wipe their hands and faces. I followed their lead.

But then I was left wondering: what now? Do we keep this towel? Is there a place to dispose of it? I didn't have to wait long. The same attendant returned, this time holding a small tray. Without needing to explain, she held it out, and I dropped the used towel into it. I'm not sure if I thanked her. Where I come from, it's not second nature to say "thank you" for every small thing someone does for you, but perhaps it should be.

Around me, not all passengers were awake. Many were still sleeping. Maybe it was the post-takeoff drinks, or maybe they just weren't interested in what was going on. A few had gotten up and stood in scattered corners of the cabin, stretching or waiting their turn for the bathroom.

Minutes later, the same attendant came by again, now pushing a cart stocked with drinks.

"What would you like to drink, sir? Soda, juice, or water?" she asked politely.

"What juices do you have?" I asked.

"Orange, apple, cranberry, or mixed," she replied, glancing at the cans in the drawer.

"Can I have orange juice?"

"Sure. With or without ice?"

"With, please."

She handed me a clear plastic cup filled two-thirds with juice and ice. Without saying a word, she reached for the tray table in front of me, unhooked it, placed a napkin and straw down, then turned her attention to the next row.

I had barely finished the juice when another attendant came along with a breakfast cart. As she approached, she asked softly, "Would you like your breakfast with omelet or veggie?"

She didn't explain what the veggie option included, and honestly, I didn't feel the need to ask. "Omelet is fine," I said.

Almost immediately, she passed me a tray packed with various items and moved on without pause.

My small table was still flat open, so I placed the tray on it and looked at the items. The tray covered the entire table. On it were a couple of covered cups, one containing a piece of cake or brownie, the other with fruit salad. There was an empty white plastic cup with a handle, something wrapped in aluminum foil (which turned out to be a large, thick piece of hot omelet nestled between two slices of bread), and several small packets containing salt, black pepper, butter, and a set of plastic cutlery, fork, knife, and spoon, along with a napkin.

Before leaving, the flight attendant extended a small empty tray toward me and asked if I would like hot coffee or tea. I placed my empty cup in the tray and replied, "Coffee would be fine, with cream and sugar, please."

For a moment, I wondered if all the hospitality was included in the price of the ticket or if I would be billed separately. But I quickly decided not to worry about it. The airline hadn't mentioned anything about additional charges, and since the Government of India (GOI) had purchased my ticket, I figured I'd ignore it unless asked for payment.

I noticed bright daylight streaming through the windows, indicating the sky had turned sunny.

After people finished their breakfasts and the attendants collected the trays, a Bollywood movie was started on the plane's central screen system. The pilot made a brief announcement about the movie, and the attendants distributed earplugs to passengers who wanted them. The lights were turned off. Though I had received the earplugs, I felt sleepy again, especially after the satisfying breakfast, so I decided not to watch the movie.

A few hours later, I woke up just in time for dinner. The pilot then reminded us that, as scheduled, the plane would make a brief stopover in London, England, to drop off some passengers and pick up others headed to Toronto, Canada. For security reasons, the pilot advised those continuing to Toronto not to leave the plane, though those who had to for any reason should take their belongings and be prepared for security clearance again. I decided to stay on board.

That's when I noticed the man I had been looking for earlier, walking back and forth in the aisles, probably stretching his legs. I approached him and started a conversation about his experience so far. Among other things, he mentioned that although he wasn't lucky enough to have an empty seat next to him, he managed to sleep through most of the flight. He expressed hope that he might get lucky during the next phase of the flight, recalling that, based on his previous experiences, fewer passengers boarded during that segment than those who disembarked.

About an hour later, new passengers started boarding. Once everyone had settled into their seats, the pilot announced we were ready to begin the next phase of the flight. I noticed the seat next to me was still vacant, which made me feel relieved.

Throughout the flight, however, there was one thing that caused some concern: the availability of bathrooms. Not only was the space tight, but with such a big crowd, there weren't enough to accommodate everyone, especially those who had urgent needs. Long lines were visible wherever you went, particularly after a drink or a heavy dinner. At one point, I noticed that most passengers were either sleeping or standing in line, waiting desperately for the bathroom to become available, while few seemed interested in the movie.

After nearly eight hours in the air since leaving London, the plane finally touched down at its final destination, Toronto International Airport, a little after 10 p.m. that same day. The landing was so smooth that almost everyone on board clapped. It took another 15-20 minutes for the plane to taxi to the assigned gate, where a gangway was connected and passengers began to disembark.

We all had to go through immigration, pick up our luggage from the belt, and clear customs. This process took about an hour in total. By a little after 11 p.m., I was out on the arrivals platform. There were cars coming in, picking up passengers and leaving. Within minutes, the crowd started to thin out.

My Extended Stopover in Toronto, Canada

While booking my flight to Winnipeg, Canada, to begin my Ph.D. studies, I noticed there were no direct flights available. Instead, I had to make a stopover either in Toronto or New York before continuing on to Winnipeg, home to the University of Manitoba. I chose Toronto, not only because it was within Canada, but also because many people from my village had already settled there and spoke highly of the city. They had often encouraged me to visit if I ever had the chance.

One of them was my classmate and close friend, whom we affectionately called Singh, or sometimes Mr. Singh. He had also made Toronto his home. Singh and I had first met in 1968 when we stood side by side in the admission line for our five-year bachelor's degree program at PAU. From that moment, we became fast friends. Over the years, he had occasionally written to me, extending an open invitation to stay with him if I ever came to Toronto.

Reading Canadian magazines in the PAU library had also piqued my interest in Toronto. The city boasted world-class attractions like the Canadian National Tower, which at the time was the tallest structure in the world, as well as Niagara Falls, the Bell Laboratories, and several renowned museums. I also learned that it was just a couple of hours' drive from the United States. So, I made up my mind to extend my stopover in Toronto for a week before heading to Winnipeg.

A week before my departure from India, I sent Singh a letter informing him of my travel plans and asking him to pick me up at the Toronto airport. I didn't have his phone number, and it never occurred to me to find it. At the time, that didn't feel like a major concern, but in hindsight, it turned out to be a significant oversight.

In the days leading up to my journey, I was overwhelmed with preparations. Between packing, securing my student visa, attending farewell parties, and meeting with friends and family, I had little time to plan my stay in Canada. Perhaps it was inexperience, or perhaps it was the influence of my parents, who always taught me not to worry too much about the future. Either way I took a leap of faith, and it was a big one.

It was just past 10 p.m. when my flight landed at Toronto International Airport. After clearing immigration and customs, I gathered my luggage onto a cart and walked through the exit, scanning the crowd for Singh. But he was nowhere in sight.

Fatigued from the long journey and growing increasingly sleepy, I started to feel anxious. I rifled through my notes, searching for any other contact I could reach. All I could find was the phone number and address of someone who had once been our neighbor in the village and had since moved to Hamilton, Ontario.

Until that night, I had never used a telephone. I had no idea how the system worked in Canada. As I fumbled with a nearby payphone, another traveler from Punjab, who had been on the same flight, noticed my struggle and came over to help. With his guidance, I tried calling the number several times, but no one answered.

Seeing my growing concern, he suggested that I take a bus to Hamilton and try calling again once I arrived there. He pointed out that the last bus of the night would be departing soon, and if I didn't make a decision quickly, I might miss it. I didn't have many options, so I agreed. He showed me where to buy a bus ticket, and fortunately, I had just enough cash left to afford it.

The man wished me good luck and walked away.

Within minutes, a bus pulled up to where I was standing with my luggage. The driver stepped off, glanced at my ticket and bags, then asked me something I couldn't understand. Maybe he spoke too quickly, or maybe it was just the unfamiliar rhythm of Canadian English. Without waiting for a response, he motioned for me to get on the bus and not worry about the luggage. Still uncertain, I hesitated, keeping close to my belongings.

He disappeared briefly to the ticket counter, then returned and saw me rooted in the same spot. Without another word, he began loading my luggage into the lower compartment of the bus. This time, I followed his lead and boarded, choosing a seat at the front so I could watch the city as we drove. The bus was nearly empty, just the driver and me.

Soon after leaving the airport, the driver picked up speed and, maybe to stay awake, started talking to me. I tried to follow, but his accent was too different, too fast. While I was confident in written English, my listening skills hadn't quite caught up, especially not with this kind of accent. I gave short answers, mostly "Yeah" or "OK", since those were the words I'd heard Canadians used often. Even when he asked where I wanted to get off in Hamilton, I replied with a noncommittal "Yeah."

Eventually, he gave up trying to converse and turned on the radio. The rest of the journey passed in silence.

Since I hadn't given him a specific destination, the driver stopped in front of a large hotel with a glowing sign that read *Royal Hotel*. He said it was the last stop before the terminal and told me to get off. He unloaded my luggage onto the sidewalk and pointed toward the hotel when I asked where I could make a phone call.

I dragged my luggage inside. It was close to 1 a.m. The hotel attendant directed me to a pay phone in the lobby. Hands trembling, I dialed the only number I had, again.

This time, someone answered. It was the neighbor from my village.

Shouting in Punjabi, I asked why he hadn't picked up earlier. He explained that he'd just returned from a birthday party and had heard the phone ring for the first time. After a quick exchange about my arrival, he asked where I was calling from. When I said the hotel name, he sounded surprised and began to wrap up the conversation, suggesting we continue the next day.

But when I told him I was only using the hotel phone and didn't have the money to stay, his tone shifted. "Why didn't you say that before?" he asked. Then he told me to wait, he'd come and pick me up.

About twenty minutes later, he arrived. I let out a long sigh of relief, silently cursing my naivety while thanking God I wasn't alone anymore.

Cancer Scare

As planned, my flight from Toronto to Winnipeg wasn't due for another week. So I asked the host family in Hamilton, the kind folks who had picked me up from the hotel the night before, if it would be alright for me to stay with them until my departure. They welcomed me warmly and said I could stay as long as I liked. With that immediate concern taken care of, I turned my attention to something that had been lingering on my mind: reconnecting with my close friend Mr. Singh, who, rather mysteriously, had failed to show up at the airport earlier.

I wrote him another letter, this time including the new address and phone number of the host family in Hamilton. Within a few days, he called. It turned out he hadn't received my previous letter because it had been mailed to an old address he'd left behind long ago. Without much preamble, he told me, actually, ordered me, to pack my things and catch the earliest bus the next morning to Scarborough, a suburb of Toronto where he lived. When I asked if he could pick me up, given that I was traveling with luggage, he simply laughed and said no. He added, almost cryptically, that he'd explain when I got there.

I brought up my upcoming connecting flight to Winnipeg, but he dismissed the concern with firm assurance, saying he'd handle the rescheduling. That was that.

The next day, I arrived at his place as directed. Only then did I come to understand why he had been unavailable and so brisk in tone. Singh was going through an incredibly difficult time. To maintain his visa status, he had to be enrolled full-time as a student, and to cover both tuition and living costs, he worked long overnight shifts. Life was a daily struggle, and he was clearly stretched thin, mentally, physically, and emotionally.

I made a casual observation about how bare the walls were in his shared home, no pictures, no decorations, no sceneries. He gave me a sharp look and said, a bit sarcastically, that he was having a hard enough time putting food on the table, and I was worried about what was on the walls. His words stung, and rightly so. I suddenly felt like a naive child.

Despite his hectic schedule, Singh went out of his way to make my brief stay memorable. He enlisted help from his local friends and relatives, including his landlord and two Indian roommates, convincing them to cook Indian food, Gobhi paranthas, for me, joking that I probably wasn't used to Canadian food yet. He even reached out to his auntie in Markham, a woman he affectionately called "Mom," and arranged for me to visit her soon.

That weekend, Singh and his friends took me sightseeing around Toronto. We visited the Great Lakes, the Canadian National Tower, the original Graham Bell Labs, and of course, the awe-inspiring Niagara Falls. The entire experience affirmed that choosing to extend my stopover in Toronto had been the right decision.

But it all took a sudden turn after our visit to Niagara Falls. I fell terribly ill and began to lose weight at an alarming rate. Lacking health insurance, I confided in Singh, who, without hesitation, let me use his medical ID card to see a doctor. Fortunately, his health card didn't carry a photo.

The doctor examined me the next morning and found signs of inflammation in my spleen and liver, though no bacteria or fungi were detected in my body fluids. He suggested a viral infection. Ironically, the diagnosis only worsened my anxiety. Having studied viruses and their possible links to cancer during my graduate and doctoral work, my mind raced toward worst-case scenarios. I couldn't help but recall the old English saying: *As knowledge doubles, so do troubles.*

Hence, the rapid loss of my weight. Another factor contributing to the decline was the growing fear that if I were to die from what I now suspected might be cancer, my friend would be the one declared dead on paper. That thought haunted me, and it troubled him just as much. If he tried to explain the truth later, it could be construed as insurance fraud, which would likely result in deportation back to India. The gravity of the situation weighed on us both. But with no clear solution, we said nothing, instead choosing to silently pray for a healthier outcome in the days ahead. I began to question whether my decision to extend the stopover in Toronto had been wise. Regret started creeping in. I should have gone straight to Winnipeg, sorted out my paperwork, obtained health insurance, and only then thought about visiting friends.

Before arriving in Canada, I had volunteered with a local doctor in my village, helping to treat patients, most commonly for malaria. That hands-on experience had given me a fair degree of confidence in recognizing its symptoms. I myself had suffered from malaria nearly every year, and I was well-versed in how it presented. So when the Canadian doctor told me he couldn't prescribe any medication due to the absence of observable bacteria or parasites in my blood, I was frustrated but not surprised. He explained that Canadian medical regulations required lab-confirmed evidence before prescribing antibiotics or anti-malarial drugs. While I respected his position, it only deepened the anxiety both my friend and I were already feeling. The possibility of cancer loomed larger. Within a week, I had lost over thirty pounds. My friend, already lean like me, had dropped fifteen. The weight loss, fed by stress, became a vicious cycle we couldn't seem to break.

Fortunately, there was one more step. The doctor had sent my blood sample to a specialized lab at the University of Toronto, the only facility nearby with an electron microscope capable of detecting organisms too small for standard equipment. A couple of days later, we received the results: the presence of malaria-related bacteria had been confirmed. Mine, as it turned out, was only the second reported case of malaria in Canadian history. The doctor called right away and told me where I could pick up the prescribed medication.

The relief was immediate and immense. I knew how to manage the drug, and within a couple of days, I felt almost normal again, tired but stable. My friend, too, recovered from the emotional toll. Soon after, I boarded my flight to Winnipeg. Once there, I completed my university enrollment, made the necessary living arrangements, and the very first thing I did was secure health insurance.

Four and a half years later, as I stood at the end of my Ph.D. journey in Winnipeg, I still carried the memories of Toronto with me, etched into my mind as if they had happened only yesterday. That chapter had given me lessons far beyond academics: humility, friendship, vulnerability, and above all, survival.

My First Thanksgiving Dinner with Canadians – a Disaster

As I landed in Winnipeg, Manitoba, I was greeted by a university staff member assigned to pick me up for my arrival at the University of Manitoba, where I was about to begin my Ph.D. program. The next morning, I completed the registration process and was introduced to the faculty and staff I would be working with, including my advisor, Dr. Cliff Bernier.

What struck me immediately was the warmth and informality of everyone I met. Unlike in India, where titles like "Doctor" or "Dr. Sahib" are used with reverence, especially in academic circles, here people insisted on using first names. When I addressed my advisor as "Dr. Bernier," he gently interrupted and asked me to simply call him "Cliff." That simple gesture, though difficult to accept at first, left a lasting impression. It made me feel not just welcome, but as though I had been accepted into a kind of academic family.

The university provided me with temporary housing on campus while I decided whether to live on or off campus. Given that I didn't know the city and had no means of transportation besides the bus, I chose to stay on campus, for the time being, it felt like the right choice.

However, living on campus came with one major drawback: the cafeteria food. While I didn't mind trying new things, my stomach hadn't adjusted yet, and I began suffering from persistent stomach aches. After about a month, I realized I couldn't continue like that. Fortunately, the university allowed me to move mid-semester on health grounds.

Before I moved out, I met another Indian student who was living alone in a two-bedroom apartment near campus. He was looking for a roommate, and I gladly moved in. With a kitchen of our own, food was no longer a problem. We cooked Indian meals regularly, and I even began acquiring a taste for Western foods like pizza, Big Macs, and Chinese takeout. I enjoyed the arrangement for a while, but soon personal issues in my roommate's life made the living situation uncomfortable, and I decided to move again.

I relocated to the basement of a nearby house, where I stayed for six months before moving once more, this time to an upstairs room in a different house. By then, I had bought a used car, which made getting around much easier and more enjoyable.

My new room was small but tidy. A slightly larger room next door was rented to another student, this one from China. We shared a compact kitchenette and a full bathroom. The landlords, a couple in their fifties who spoke both English and French, lived on the main floor. The finished basement was not rented out, but they allowed me to use it for a few hours at a time, particularly when entertaining guests, as long as I left it clean afterward.

The rent was very affordable, and over time I came to understand why. The couple enjoyed traveling to visit their daughters and relatives across Canada and valued having someone in the house while they were away more than earning rent. Though the kitchen lacked a formal sink, and I had to use the bathroom sink or the tub for washing dishes and collecting water, I quickly adapted. Occasionally, they would let me use their main kitchen downstairs, especially if I had company and they weren't using it themselves.

That house became my home for the rest of my time in Winnipeg. It was simple, yet it gave me a sense of stability and belonging that lasted throughout my Ph.D. journey.

Just before arriving in Winnipeg, I had heard about a man named Dr. Khangura. He had earned a Ph.D. from PAU, recently moved to Canada, and was living in Winnipeg with his wife and two-year-old son. I'd never met him, so I was hesitant to reach out. To my surprise, he called me instead.

When I asked how he came to know about me, he said, "I have my sources in India." Then with a chuckle, he added, "Apparently, everyone on the PAU campus knows about you, the guy who won the National Scholarship for Study Abroad and is heading to Winnipeg. That's you, right?" I confirmed, a little flattered, and thanked him for calling.

He soon invited me over for dinner during an upcoming holiday. I accepted. After a few phone calls and visits, we became close friends. His family welcomed me warmly, and we spent a lot of time together. He managed a local field hockey club, sponsored by the Manitoba province, and invited me to join. Since my home was along the route to the field, he offered to pick me up regularly. On those drives, he would sometimes let me practice driving his car, even helping me get my first driver's license.

Outside his family, though, I had no other social connections. I wanted to learn the Canadian English accent and understand local customs to better integrate, but no opportunity came, until one day in October, just before Canadian Thanksgiving.

My landlords, who lived downstairs, asked if I was free to join their family dinner. They mentioned that their three daughters and one son-in-law would be there. Eager for a chance to experience something new and connect with locals, I said yes right away. When I asked what time, the lady said, "Six pm. Is that okay?" "Yes," I replied, "That works."

I was excited and began counting down the days. In the meantime, Dr. Khangura also invited me to his home for Thanksgiving. I apologized and explained I was already committed.

On Thanksgiving Day, I didn't want to risk traffic delays, so I left my lab early and got home by 5:00 pm. The driveway was already lined with cars, and I could hear the chatter from downstairs. But instead of heading down, I went to my room.

Something in me, perhaps an ingrained cultural instinct, said, *Don't go yet.* In India, arriving on time, especially at a social gathering, can be seen as overeager, even rude. Guests often let the host wait a little, sometimes even for hours. So I waited, watching the clock, each minute dragging. Finally, at 6:00 pm, I stood up, but again hesitated. I didn't want to seem desperate for food or company. I waited another 15 minutes, trying to convince myself it was the polite thing to do. When I finally went downstairs, I found everyone already at the dinner table, and nearly finished. Embarrassed, I struggled to come up with an excuse: traffic, work, unexpected calls. But none of them felt convincing. So I simply said I was tired and had fallen asleep.

They were kind and said it was no problem, that there was still plenty of food. But I felt disappointed. I had hoped to learn something about Canadian customs, how people eat, how they talk, how they celebrate. Now I'd missed the conversations, the laughter, the warmth of sharing a meal together. Worse, I didn't recognize most of the food: turkey, stuffing, foil-wrapped baked potatoes, different kinds of pies. I didn't know how to serve myself or even where to begin.

So I stuck to the familiar, corn and a potato, and politely claimed stomach issues to avoid explaining my discomfort. Soon, people began saying their goodbyes. I thanked the hosts and slipped back upstairs, where I spent the rest of the night thinking about how foolish I'd been.

That night taught me a lesson I've never forgotten. Ever since, whenever I'm invited somewhere, I show up on time, sometimes even a few minutes early. It lets me fully enjoy the food, the company, and the conversations. And, more often than not, the hosts appreciate it. I've learned that in this part of the world, being punctual is not desperation, it's respect.

Ice Skating, "Again?"

Born and raised in Punjab, India, I had experienced the crispness of winter and seen a bit of frost, but I had never encountered real snow or ice, despite living just a hundred miles south of the world-famous Himalayas, home to snow-covered peaks and frozen landscapes. The closest I ever came to witnessing snowfall was through the romanticized scenes in Bollywood films.

So, when I arrived in Winnipeg toward the end of August 1977, I was filled with anticipation. Everyone I met, whether at my residence, in class, or among the new friends I was making, spoke of the long, brutal winters ahead. Their advice came in a steady stream: be prepared for heavy snowfall and subfreezing temperatures, avoid staying out too long in the cold, watch out for icy sidewalks, make sure your car has a working block heater, never forget to plug it in during winter, and always keep a shovel and booster cables in your trunk.

My lab technician offered some calm reassurance one day. "It's normal to feel anxious," he said. "But don't worry too much. You'll always find someone to help, just make sure to ask."

It didn't take long before winter arrived in full force. Around November 20, a massive storm swept through Winnipeg. The news called it a blizzard. By the next morning, every car parked outside was completely buried. The roads vanished under deep snow, impassable for both vehicles and pedestrians.

Looking out the window, I asked my landlady where her car was. She glanced outside and, without missing a beat, said, "It's right next to yours," meaning she couldn't see hers either. It was as if a thick white sheet had fallen from the sky and swallowed everything in sight. The world outside had frozen into stillness. For a moment, all of life pressed pause.

But to my surprise, as soon as the snow stopped falling, the city sprang into action. Snowplows and massive cleaning equipment hit the streets, clearing major roads within a couple of days. Buses resumed service, and cautiously, wearing snow boots and choosing public transport over driving, I made my way to the university campus.

There, I discovered a curious secret to surviving winter: the university buildings were connected through a network of underground tunnels. As long as I stayed below ground, life on campus felt almost normal. But above ground, the weather dominated every conversation. While waiting at a bus stop one evening, I asked a fellow commuter how long winter would last. He smiled and said, "Don't worry, it's only nine months. The rest is summer."

That sense of humor seemed essential for surviving the cold. Another thing caught my eye on campus, many people had a pair of ice skates slung casually over their shoulders. I asked someone about it, and he said, "You better get used to it. Ice skating makes it easier, and safer, to get around. Plus, it's fun."

He wasn't joking. In Winnipeg, skating wasn't just a winter activity, it was a way of life, something close to a cultural ritual. Someone suggested I could rent skates at the local rink instead of buying them, and maybe give it a try. In that moment, I realized that winter in this part of the world wasn't just something to endure, it was something people embraced.

One day, while we were chatting about ice-skating, Kelly, a cheerful staff member from my lab, offered to take me to a local rink and teach me the basics. I accepted with no hesitation. Before leaving, someone in the lab jokingly warned me that it was easy to fall and break a bone, so I should be extra careful. I laughed it off. Determined as ever, I was ready to face the ice.

The moment I stepped into the rink, I was struck by the lively scene. The ice stretched out in a wide oval, gleaming under the lights. Skaters moved steadily in a single direction to the rhythm of loud, upbeat music. Some looked just as hesitant as I felt, first-timers clinging to the railing or wobbling unsteadily. Others, however, seemed like seasoned performers, confidently weaving through the crowd, crossing one foot over the other with fluid ease as they passed on either side.

Despite my nerves, I couldn't help but feel a pull toward the ice. Kelly helped me into a pair of rental skates, tightening the laces and checking the fit with practiced hands. Then, gently taking one of mine in hers, she led me toward the skating floor.

My first day going for ice skating in Winnipeg, Canada

Skating itself wasn't new to me; I had already tried roller-skating before. But ice-skating was something entirely different, challenging and, to be honest, a bit scary. Still, with Kelly holding my hand, I picked it up quickly. She was impressed by how fast I was catching on. After just two or three laps around the rink, I felt confident enough to go on my own and let go of her hand. It was a mistake, a bit premature, I soon realized.

An experienced skater, moving quickly in a zig-zag, cut in front of me, and I lost my balance. Just as I was about to fall,

I remembered what someone had warned me earlier: I could easily break my arm or leg. So, instinctively, I protected my limbs but let my face go forward. The impact was sharp, and I hurt myself badly.

Kelly saw me fall and rushed over immediately. She looked concerned, pointing to a red patch on the ice where I had landed, and told me I needed medical attention right away, my face was bleeding. There was a clinic not far from the rink, connected by an underground tunnel, so I got there quickly. The doctor stitched up the gash above my right eye, five or six stitches in all. He told me I was lucky it didn't affect my eye and advised me to stay off the ice for at least three weeks to allow the wound to heal properly.

But less than a week later, I felt the pull to return to the rink. Having played various sports since my school days, I was proud of my athleticism, perhaps too proud. I ignored the doctor's advice and went back, determined to prove I wasn't timid. Naturally, I fell again, and once more, it was my face that took the hit, this time, my chin. To my bad luck, the same doctor was on duty. When he saw me, he sighed and exclaimed, "Again?" I just smiled sheepishly as he stitched up my chin, four stitches this time.

Despite my stubbornness, I didn't give up. I kept returning to the rink, learning not just how to skate but how to fall safely. Over time, my skills improved, and I decided to buy my own skates. Then, one day, I saw a group of kids playing ice hockey in an open park. One of them asked me if I wanted to join. "What the heck," I thought, and joined in. With a borrowed hockey stick, I tried my hand at the game.

It was a historic moment for me, even if the game ended soon after. I wasn't sure if I'd kept up with the kids, but I was overjoyed nonetheless.

The next day, when I told the staff in my lab, especially Kelly, about my impromptu hockey game, they were stunned. They couldn't believe it.

Pizza Delivery – A Lesson for Life

Before coming to Winnipeg, Canada, I had no idea how expensive it would be to live there. I assumed that the scholarship I had earned would cover all my basic expenses, but in reality, it did not. One reason for my ignorance was that I didn't know anyone who had won the Government of India scholarship and gone to Winnipeg to pursue a Ph.D. I had no one to discuss financial conditions with before my arrival. Another reason was that the harsh winters, where temperatures often dropped to minus 40 degrees Celsius in January and February, made people in India hesitant to move there. As a result, there was no one back home to provide the detailed information I needed about living costs in Winnipeg.

Like many others from Punjab, I also had ambitions beyond just surviving in Canada. I wanted to earn money to support my parents back in India, who were struggling to pay off debts and repair their home. I assumed that employment opportunities in Canada would be better than those in India. So, I decided to look for part-time work, hoping to earn extra money to help my family.

I reached out to my friend in Winnipeg, Dr. Khangura, to ask if he could guide me in finding a job that I could do in the evenings. Coincidentally, he was already working part-time as a pizza delivery driver. He told me about the job and seemed confident I would have no trouble getting hired, since the restaurant was always busy and had a "help wanted" sign out for new drivers. However, he couldn't be sure until he spoke to the manager, which he planned to do that evening.

The following day, around 5 p.m., Dr. Khangura took me to the pizza place and introduced me to the manager. The manager asked me to wait until he was finished with the customers. After a brief orientation about the job and the pay I would receive at the end of my shift, he apologized for being busy and turned to my friend to fill in the details. The store was packed with customers, and the phones were ringing non-stop.

After about 20 minutes of waiting, I finally got my turn. I was nervous, having barely gotten used to pizzas, let alone delivering them in an unfamiliar area. My friend noticed my anxiety and reassured me, saying, "The worst that can happen is that he (the manager) lets you go."

The guy at the counter handed me the order slips for four customers and reminded me that I had 45 minutes from the order time on the slips to make all the deliveries. My friend lent me his extra map of the area until I could get my own. I picked up all the pizzas and set off, feeling excited about my first job in Canada.

Because of the cold weather, I had put on a down-filled jacket, but the pizzas were hot and the car had an electric oven to keep them warm. Soon, I was sweating. As it was getting dark, I parked near the first customer's address and tried to figure out the location on the map. The address was in an apartment complex, and I wasted a lot of time finding the right building. When I finally arrived, I knocked on the door. The man who opened it looked at the pizza in my hand and said he didn't need it anymore.

I asked if he had ordered one, and he confirmed that he had, but it was past the 45-minute delivery window. He didn't want it anymore. I left the building, called the manager from a phone booth, and explained the situation. The manager told me to return to the store with the undelivered pizzas.

On my way back, I started to panic. I realized that since the pizzas were past the 45-minute window, that was probably why the manager didn't want me to finish the deliveries. I had failed to do my job correctly. I couldn't stop thinking, "What excuse should I give to the manager? Or maybe I should just hand over the car keys and leave without saying anything." I arrived at the pizza place, bracing myself to be fired.

Upon reaching the pizza place, the manager told me to put all the pizzas I had brought back on a table in the back room and then take a seat on the bench where customers would wait for their carry-out pizzas. I took this as a sign that it was only a matter of time before he let me go. Half an hour passed. The other drivers would come in, glance at me, and smile in a way that made me feel they all knew exactly what had happened with the pizzas I was supposed to deliver. It was becoming increasingly uncomfortable sitting there.

"If he wants to fire me, why isn't he doing it already?" I wondered to myself. I also started feeling embarrassed about what my friend might think. "He must be thinking, what kind of person am I, a scholar who won a prestigious scholarship in India, yet can't even do a simple job?" I couldn't shake the thought.

Finally, the manager came over. He asked me to get up, placed his right arm around my shoulders, and said, "Let's go inside." Apologizing for the cluttered state of his office, he pointed me to a chair and pulled another one for himself, sitting very close to me. Nervously, though I wanted to leave, I forced myself into the chair.

He began by apologizing for taking so long and for not having properly trained me. "Paul," he said, "I want to make it clear that you shouldn't worry about the pizzas or the customers. I've already fixed things by sending out free hot pizzas once I learned you couldn't make the delivery on time. As for the other drivers, believe me, they weren't laughing at you. They were laughing at themselves, remembering their own awkward first days here. Don't worry about them. They're not half as intelligent as you are."

The manager then shared some practical tips: "While waiting for pizzas to be ready, check the map on the wall behind you. Make notes about how to get to delivery addresses, gather everything that's been ordered, pizzas and all, and then pick up the pizzas. Trust me, spending ten minutes on the map here will save you at least half an hour on the road."

He stood up, signaling it was time to get back to work.

I felt a wave of relief wash over me, an understatement. It was as if a huge weight had been lifted. I had never had a manager speak to me like that before, especially after I had messed up so badly. It was my first big impression of Canadians: "A manager can be this down-to-earth!" It seemed almost unbelievable. He wasn't focused on the loss; he cared more about protecting my honor by speaking with me privately. I hadn't expected that level of consideration, even from my friends. From that day forward, I made sure to remember every word he said.

Within a week, I became the top pizza delivery driver and the highest earner among them. I was so efficient at delivering pizzas on time that I ended up making more money in tips than from wages alone. But more than the money, the lessons the manager taught me stayed with me. A few months later, I was selected to be an assistant teacher at my university and quit my job at the pizza place. The lessons I had learned there became an integral part of me. Even today, years later, I still use those lessons. When I go somewhere for the first time, I always check the map first, print directions in case my phone dies, and make sure everything essential is ready the night before I leave. In the forty-plus years I've worked in universities and the federal government, I can't recall ever being late except for reasons beyond my control, like bad weather, traffic jams, accidents, or health emergencies.

My First Encounter with Police in the USA

Two days before Christmas in 1979, a friend of mine, Dr. Khangura, who had invited me to his home on major holidays, shared an idea for celebrating Christmas differently that year. When I asked him what he meant, he explained that he was thinking of driving to Minneapolis, Minnesota, USA. His reasoning was simple: (a) the weather forecast looked favorable for a long trip, and (b) he had recently bought a new car and hadn't yet taken his family on a proper trip. He hadn't discussed the idea with his family yet, but wanted to check with me first to see if I was available and interested.

Although he had other friends and relatives in Winnipeg, he chose to ask me because, for months, I had been urging him to visit the United States, somewhere I had never been, and his family was comfortable with my driving and preferred that I not pry into their personal matters. I readily accepted.

The family was initially hesitant, given the unpredictable weather forecast, but I convinced them by suggesting that we could always turn around if the weather worsened. Once everyone agreed, we were so excited that we decided to leave Winnipeg early the next morning, on Christmas Eve.

I had driven Dr. Khangura's new car on several occasions, so I was very comfortable behind the wheel. When he picked me up the next day and handed me the car keys, I understood immediately and took them without hesitation.

Nine hours later, we arrived in Minneapolis, just as nightfall settled over the city. As we drove through downtown, we were all thrilled by the sight of towering buildings, beautifully decorated for Christmas. Although Winnipeg wasn't a small town, and its downtown was equally festive, I had never visited during the Christmas season at night. This was my first time experiencing the sparkling streetlights, decorations on the large buildings, and displays inside The Mall of America. It felt as though we had stepped into another world, like we were in heaven.

After spending two to three hours sightseeing and enjoying a lovely dinner at a revolving restaurant in the tallest building, we were exhausted and eager to find a place to rest. We started calling hotels, only to learn that all of them were fully booked. We then tried motels from the phone directory, but they too had no vacancies. The family's gaze shifted to me, as if silently questioning why I hadn't thought to make reservations in advance. Meanwhile, the child began to cry softly, and the cold of the evening started to sink in. We were desperate.

With no options left, we decided to keep driving, thinking that not all motels advertise in the directory and that perhaps we could find a vacancy somewhere. But luck was not on our side. We checked a few more places, only to find that all were full. To make matters worse, we were running out of ideas. The weather was too harsh to spend the night in the car, and we had already been in it for almost twelve hours. Tired, frustrated, and cranky, we were at our wit's end.

Then, an idea came to me. I remembered from the map that a YMCA (Young Men's Christian Association) wasn't far from where we were. I mentioned to the family that they often had rooms available, especially in winter when fewer tourists visited places like Minneapolis. The family liked the idea and urged me to check it out.

It was close to midnight by the time we arrived at the YMCA. There were no lights visible through the front windows, so we decided to try the back entrance. Thankfully, we saw a light coming from the large glass windows. We parked the car nearby and approached the window. As we knocked, an elderly white man inside came close, but his words were inaudible. We gestured to indicate that we were looking for rooms, and although we couldn't be sure if he understood, he raised both hands in a gesture that seemed to say, "Wait here." He nodded and walked back into a room. We interpreted his actions as a signal that he would check on room availability and return shortly.

We continued waiting by the window for about ten minutes when, suddenly, we heard a loud voice from behind: "Can we help you with something?" We turned around to see two tall, muscular officers in police uniforms. They were much bigger than us, and we were completely taken aback.

As I tried to explain that we were from Canada and… one of the officers interrupted, saying, "Yes, we saw your license plate, but what exactly are you trying to do here?"

I told him that we were looking for two rooms for the night but hadn't been able to find any. We had hoped the YMCA might have availability. The officer instructed us to return to our car and wait there.

As we sat in the car, Dr. Khangura, attempting to lighten the mood, joked, "We couldn't find rooms outside, but at least we'll definitely get rooms inside now, locked up in jail." I didn't respond.

A few moments later, another police car arrived, and one of the officers came over to us. He asked us to follow his car. "The motel we're taking you to has two rooms available," he said. "You can check them out, and if they don't work for you, we'll take you to another one nearby that also has rooms."

Without hesitation, we all said together, "They should be fine."

The officer insisted, "No, you need to check them first and make sure everything you need is there."

In just five minutes, we arrived at the motel. I went inside to inquire about room availability and the rent. The clerk provided all the information we needed and even showed us the rooms. We were all pleased with what we saw. I went back outside, told the officers that the family liked the rooms, and thanked them profusely.

"Are you sure?" one of the officers asked.

"Yes, sir. We really appreciate your help," I replied.

The officers nodded and drove off.

There are no words to describe how relieved we were. After signing the papers, we hurried to our rooms. We were so exhausted, we didn't even have the energy to sit and talk.

The next morning, we spent the entire morning reflecting on how amazing the police in the U.S. had been, especially compared to what we'd heard about them in Canada or our experiences with law enforcement in India. That night, we learned a valuable lesson: never go to a place without making hotel reservations, especially during the holiday season.

"What's in it for Me?"

It was in the spring of 1980 when a high-ranking official from India approached me to discuss something private. At the time, I was the president of the Indian Students Association (ISA), representing students from India at the University of Manitoba (U of M) in Winnipeg, Canada. He introduced himself as Dr. Reddy, a director of animal husbandry for the State Government of Andhra Pradesh. He also mentioned that he had a doctorate in animal sciences and was visiting the U of M on a sabbatical assignment for a year. His strong southern Indian English accent and mid-fifties appearance made him seem dignified, yet somewhat out of place in the foreign surroundings.

Dr. Reddy explained that he was struggling with both food and cultural shock. He wondered if I could help him find another Indian student who could share his food and living space, easing his sense of isolation. He confided that if he could not find a roommate, he might cancel his sabbatical and return to India.

I could understand his predicament. Two years prior, I had experienced similar challenges, so I was sympathetic to his situation. I told him I would do my best to help and asked for a couple of days to look into possible solutions.

I contacted as many Indian friends as I could, hoping to find someone willing to share their living space and cook Indian food with him. Unfortunately, most of my contacts were from Punjab or other regions, not Andhra Pradesh, and none were interested. The differences in age and language seemed to matter more to them than I had anticipated.

Determined to assist Dr. Reddy, I saw no other option but to offer him a place in my own living arrangement. My room was small, about 8' by 8', situated upstairs in a house where the owners lived on the main floor. The setup wasn't ideal, outside my room was a small table for kitchen items, a stove, and a small fridge in the hallway. There was no formal kitchen, no sink for washing dishes, and no water source nearby except for the bathroom, which I shared with a Chinese student renting another room across from mine.

Despite the cramped space, Dr. Reddy immediately assured me that although he had never cooked before, he was eager to learn and would help with the cooking. Given that he was only staying for a few months, I told him not to worry about groceries or contributing to the rent, I enjoyed cooking, and it would be my pleasure to handle it all. Out of courtesy, I informed the landlord about Dr. Reddy's temporary stay, offering to cover any additional rent or charges. However, the landlords simply shrugged it off, saying it wasn't their concern and I didn't need to worry about it.

Before Dr. Reddy arrived, I had been living alone. With no TV and at a time when computers and iPads had yet to emerge, I often found myself bored, looking for things outside the house to keep me busy. I would visit friends, go swimming, or play sports. Other times, I'd talk to friends or members of the ISA. To make this easier, I had connected my phone to a 25-foot-long cord, so I could take it with me anywhere on the floor.

When Dr. Reddy moved in as my new roommate, simply having someone to talk to and visit places with made my days much more enjoyable. The only challenge was that we needed to communicate in English. Initially, we both struggled a bit with each other's accents, but soon enough, it wasn't an issue. We even started to enjoy speaking English, it became a fun way to improve our vocabulary.

One evening, as we were cooking dinner and chatting, I noticed the landlady, Ms. Simone, coming upstairs. I assumed that we were talking too loudly and quickly gestured to Dr. Reddy to tone it down. She approached us and, in a soft voice, said, "Paul, I didn't mean to interrupt, but I heard you two speaking English. I just wanted to let you know that we don't mind if you speak your own language instead. After all, we're from France, and we often speak French unless we're talking to someone who only speaks English."

I smiled and replied, "Thank you, Ms. Simone, but we're not speaking in English for you. It's just that English is the only language we can use to communicate. Dr. Reddy comes from a region in southern India where the language is Telugu, and I'm from northern India where we speak Punjabi. So, English is our common ground. But I really appreciate you saying that." She smiled and left us to continue our cooking.

As time passed, we grew so accustomed to seeing each other daily that when one of us didn't come home at the expected time, the other would miss them and start wondering what had happened. Dr. Reddy didn't have a Manitoba driver's license, nor did he intend to get one. His reasoning was that since he was only there for a few months, he didn't need a car for work. He'd already bought a monthly bus pass, which was cheaper than maintaining a car. However, I had told him that as long as we shared a similar schedule at the U of M, I didn't mind giving him a ride. It saved him both time and money, and that became our routine every day.

One weekend, after playing field hockey, I came home and noticed that Dr. Reddy wasn't there. I knew he had the day off, so I figured he might be out walking or shopping nearby. Hours passed, and he still hadn't returned, which started to worry me. Unable to do much else, I decided to take a nap. When I woke up, I found him sitting in a chair with a tabloid newspaper, the kind you'd typically find at a bus station.

As soon as he saw me stir, he started the conversation.:

Dr. Reddy (DR): "Did you have a long day? You look tired."

Me: "No, I just decided to rest. I didn't have anything else to do. Where have you been? I was looking for you."

DR: "Oh, I decided to use that stupid bus pass I bought for the whole month but hadn't used once, since I've been riding with you everywhere. So before it expired, I figured I'd make use of it."

Me: "You mean you spent the whole day riding different buses so the pass would be used up?"

DR: "No, not different buses. I just sat on the same bus all day, going round and round."

I couldn't help it, I laughed. How could he use up the whole bus pass just by riding the same bus? I wondered, but decided not to comment on it. It was time to focus on cooking and other things, so I changed the topic.

Me: "By the way, your friend from Brandon called again a few times."

DR: "Did you pick up the phone? What did you tell him this time?"

Me: "Same old, told him you're not home and that I'll let him know when you return."

DR: "Oh, good."

Me: "I have a question. Your friend has been calling almost every day, and each time, you tell me not to pick up or to lie to him with a different excuse. What's going on?"

He went silent for a few minutes. When I looked at him and repeated the question, he sighed and finally spoke.

DR: "I know this guy from our college days. He's also from Andhra Pradesh. He came to Canada a few years ago and has been living in Brandon ever since. Brandon is about 250 kilometers, or 150 miles, west of Winnipeg. But we've kept in touch, and we often meet when he visits his relatives in India."

Me: "Is that it? But why don't you want to talk to him?"

DR: "It's not that. He has a daughter who is about to finish her MD here in Canada, and he wants her to marry my son, who is already an MD and practicing in India. They're the same age, or maybe my son is a year older."

Me: "That sounds good to me. What's the problem? Do you not like her, or is it your son who doesn't like her?"

DR: "Everything is fine, match-wise. But there's one issue that really bothers me, and that's why I'm not interested in this arrangement."

Me: "One issue?"

DR: "Yes. What's in it for me? That's the issue. If my son marries someone in India, according to tradition, I'll get at least Rs 200,000 in dowry, more if the girl's parents are very rich. I'll get nothing if the marriage happens here. The guy is very miserly. I know him well."

Me: "Wow. And that cash in dowry is really that important to you?"

DR: "Of course."

The dinner was ready, so we stopped talking. I had no interest in discussing that issue anymore, or any issue for that matter. We finished our meal quickly and headed straight to bed.

Soon, Dr. Reddy was asleep, but I struggled to drift off. I kept thinking about how greedy and selfish he was. He didn't care about the future of his son, his friend in Brandon, or his friend's daughter. It was all about the dowry he would get if his son married in India instead of Canada. What happened to that idea that educated people help change society for the better? Eventually, I either stopped hearing Dr. Reddy snoring or maybe I fell asleep myself.

The next morning, I told Dr. Reddy I had some errands to run, so I wouldn't be going to the university. That meant he had no choice but to take the bus. When he returned, I told him that the landlady downstairs had come up after he left and said, "Your friend has overstayed as a guest and needs to move out immediately." I knew I was lying, but I had no choice. I couldn't stand him anymore.

Taking our phone outside the room, Dr. Reddy dialed a few numbers and spoke to some people in Telugu. About an hour later, someone pulled up in a car, picked him up, and drove away. No words were exchanged. Just like that, his friend in Brandon also stopped calling.

Representing Manitoba in Field Hockey

Playing different sports had always been my hobby since childhood, and I continued with it through schools and colleges, whether in India or abroad. As a child, I was particularly keen on playing field hockey. Since my parents could not afford to buy me a hockey stick, I would often take my father's walking cane, which he used to protect himself from stray dogs, and play with the other kids in the neighborhood. Many of the other children were in the same boat financially, so using walking canes as hockey sticks became a common, accepted practice.

My parents would often discourage me from playing hockey, mainly because they believed (a) it would take my attention away from schoolwork, and (b) if I got hurt, which kids often did, they wouldn't be able to afford the treatment. When kids' canes broke, some would cry, giving their parents an opportunity to ground them and keep them from playing for days. I went through that cycle until I learned to make my own sticks from dead twigs.

As I grew older, my interests shifted. I took up diving and swimming in a nearby river, and later, I played volleyball, ping pong (or table tennis), carom, and chess. After moving to Canada, I spent my spare time either playing badminton or swimming in the university pool until someone introduced me to roller-skating, ice-skating, and, once again, field hockey. Since I had played field hockey in my childhood, it quickly became my favorite sport again.

My constant practice over the next two years paid off in 1980 when I was selected to play for the Manitoba team in an interprovincial tournament in Vancouver, a Canada-level national event. I never thought of myself as one of the best players. In India, I might not have even made it onto my school's team, let alone the college team. Yet, in Manitoba, the story was different. The province's men's field hockey team was still in its early stages, and it took only some experience to be selected.

The biggest advantage for me was the opportunity to travel across Canada at no cost, from the east coast to the west. I also had the honor of playing alongside Trevor Porritt, who later went on to play for the Canada men's national field hockey team in the 1984 and 1988 Summer Olympics. Trevor was the top scorer for the gold medal-winning Canadian team at the 1987 Pan American Games and was inducted into the Manitoba Sports Hall of Fame in 2000.

My only regret was that, as usual, I never bothered to save photos of that experience. Fortunately, the person who first took me to the team had taken a photo and kindly shared it with me nearly 40 years later. I'm forever grateful for that. In the photo, I'm sitting, encircled.

Members of field hockey team representing Manitoba province in Canadian tournament in 1980

In May 1982, I completed the requirements for my Ph.D. and left Canada for good. With that, my time playing sports there, especially field hockey, came to an end. A couple of months later, I returned to Michigan in the United States, where my athletic interests gradually shifted. Men's field hockey had little to no following in that region, so I turned to racquetball, squash, and tennis instead. These indoor sports not only filled the gap left by field hockey, but also fit well with my new environment and lifestyle.

Cruising to Vancouver Island, British Columbia

If I recall correctly, it was the summer of 1981 when I decided to visit the city of Vancouver, British Columbia. I had been there once before, about a year earlier, as part of the Manitoba field hockey team, but that trip left little time for sightseeing beyond the playing fields and whatever stops our team itinerary included. This time, a friend from Winnipeg, Jasbir, invited me to accompany him on a trip to visit his relative who lived in Vancouver. I eagerly agreed. I had long dreamed of seeing the city's famed natural beauty.

I remembered someone once describing Vancouver as "a place for the newly-weds or the nearly-deads," meaning it was a favorite destination either for honeymooners or retirees with enough resources to enjoy a relaxed and comfortable life. That saying stuck with me. I had also heard about the city's strong Sikh presence, which included several historic Gurdwaras, a Khalsa School, and a successful Khalsa Credit Union. These institutions had made Vancouver well known among Sikhs, even in India.

British Columbia, true to its name, was one of the early regions in Canada where British settlers arrived and later brought Sikh laborers from Punjab to assist with farming and other work. Vancouver also held historical significance as the port of arrival for the Komagata Maru, a Japanese steamship that carried 376 Sikh passengers from India. Suspected by the British government of being revolutionaries, they were denied entry into Canada in 1914 and forced to remain at sea for over a month. Eventually, under political pressure, Canadian authorities turned the ship back. Upon its return to India on September 26, 1914, British forces reportedly opened fire before the passengers could disembark, fearing bad publicity. Many were killed onboard. That tragic incident further fueled my desire to see Vancouver. When Jasbir extended the invitation, I didn't have to think twice.

We began our journey with a stop in Calgary, then took a train to Edmonton and marveled at the breathtaking views of the Rocky Mountains along the way. From there, we continued to Vancouver by bus. The entire trip took about a week, and once we arrived, we decided to rent a car so we could explore at our own pace. Surrounded by mountains, rivers, and the Pacific Ocean, Vancouver was everything I had imagined, full of natural wonders and a spirit of adventure.

Among other highlights, we visited downtown, Stanley Park, and several notable Gurdwaras, including the Khalsa Diwan Society and Gurdwara Singh Sabha. We also stopped by the Khalsa School and North Vancouver. Jasbir's relative, who was hosting us, insisted that no trip would be complete without visiting Vancouver Island, especially the cities of Victoria, the capital of British Columbia, and Nanaimo. He told us that the ferry to the island could carry vehicles on its lower decks and that we'd need to arrive at least an hour early if we wanted to board with our car.

The next day, we arrived at the ferry terminal and were surprised by the scale of the ship. Despite the term "ferry," it was a massive, multilevel vessel. Dozens of vehicles waited in four or five lanes, and guides directed drivers where to park once aboard. Instructions were clear: turn off your engine, leave the keys in the ignition, and follow the signs upstairs. Many walk-on passengers had already parked in nearby lots and boarded on foot.

Once the ship was fully loaded, the crew untied it, and we began to move, slowly but steadily. It was a bright and sunny afternoon. Most passengers gathered in open areas to enjoy the stunning views that made Vancouver so beloved. Some took photos, while others simply stood quietly, soaking in the coastal breeze and mountainous scenery. We later learned that many of the passengers were locals commuting between the mainland and the island for work. It was a revelation to us, what we saw as a once-in-a-lifetime sightseeing adventure was, for them, just another day.

An hour and a half later, the ferry reached its destination. It took another thirty minutes before we could retrieve our car and disembark. Once back on the road, we spent the rest of the day exploring, driving in and around Victoria, pausing here and there to enjoy the sights. We visited the downtown area, took in the charm of the historic buildings, had dinner at a cozy restaurant, and eventually checked into a hotel just outside the town.

Victoria had a quiet grace to it, a restful kind of beauty. Unlike the fast-paced rhythm of large cities, it invited you to slow down. Everything seemed well-kept and thoughtfully preserved, with a gentle atmosphere that made the visit feel like a step back in time. We were glad to have brought the car; there was far more to see than we could have managed on foot during our short half-day stay.

We noticed many tourists opting for horse-drawn carriage rides, guided tours that meandered through the streets, highlighting the city's heritage architecture. It added a quaint charm, and we could see the appeal, an elegant way to take in the history and ambiance of the place.

The next morning, we drove toward neighboring towns like Nanaimo, curious to see what life looked like in the mountainous and coastal regions of the island. The natural landscape was stunning, largely untouched, its raw beauty left intact.

By late afternoon, we boarded the ferry back to Vancouver, carrying with us the quiet memory of Victoria's peaceful allure.

Chapter IV – My Life in USA

Finally, I Got a Job Offer

As anticipated, I completed my Ph.D. degree requirements in May of 1982.

Convocation conferring Ph.D. degree to me in May. 1982, in Winnipeg, Canada

Immediately afterward, I left Canada for India in June, in accordance with the terms of the Government of India scholarship program that had largely funded my education. Months prior, anticipating this move, I had written to several institutions in India, including my alma mater, Punjab

Agricultural University (PAU), inquiring about possible job openings.

Dr. Bedi, the Head of the Department of Plant Pathology and someone who knew me well from my master's program, responded warmly. He appreciated my reaching out at what he called "an opportune time." A position for a Plant Virologist had just opened in his department, he said, and he assured me that he would keep it for me, provided I arrived by the end of June 1982.

Encouraged by his response, I made every effort to return as early as possible. I met Dr. Bedi in the second week of June. But to my shock, everything fell apart. The job he had promised was gone. Worse still, he would not offer even a temporary role, such as a Research Fellowship, to help me bridge the gap until something more permanent could be found.

When I showed him the letter he had written, all it did was compel him to admit, somewhat sheepishly, that political pressure had forced him to fill the position with someone else, someone who wasn't even a virologist, just days before I arrived.

Disappointed and disillusioned, I tried applying elsewhere in India, but it became painfully clear that in the absence of powerful connections or political backing, doors remained firmly closed. My academic credentials, years of hard work, top ranks, even being one of the thirty scholars selected out of millions, seemed to count for very little.

My parents and extended family were bewildered. They asked me endless questions I had no answers for. My father, who had always believed in merit and effort, asked in quiet disbelief, "How is it possible that someone like you, with such achievements, can't even get an entry-level job?"

I met his eyes, but I had no words. His frustration was mine too. The belief I had clung to for so long, that education alone could lift someone out of poverty, had begun to crack.

In a final attempt, I decided to travel to New Delhi to meet with a senior official at the Ministry of Education, the same person who had corresponded with me throughout the scholarship process and had often described himself as my point of contact for any post-study matters.

My thinking was simple: if the government had invested so much in scholars like me, surely it had some mechanism for employment or repayment. But I was wrong.

The official, though polite, denied the existence of any such program. He promised only to keep my file open and said he would inform me if anything suitable came up within the Ministry or government-funded agricultural institutions. He also added, with a shrug of realism, that seeking a postdoctoral position elsewhere, whether in India or abroad, would be entirely acceptable and consistent with the rules of the scholarship.

His candor, however, shocked me even more than his indifference.

"Sir," I asked, "if the Government of India spends so much money sending scholars abroad, don't you have any plan for utilizing that investment?"

He looked around, lowered his voice, and said, "Strictly between us, India has too many Ph.D.s already. Dig anywhere in the ground and you'll find one. So how can we absorb them all?"

He tried to soften the blow. "I'll keep your file active. If something comes up, I'll let you know. But if you find a position outside, inform me so I can ensure you're protected."

The message couldn't have been clearer. I left.

When I got home, everyone was full of questions. "So, what happened? Did you get a job? Are you moving to Delhi?"

Some, half-joking, prodded further: "Are you joining the Central Government now?"

I smiled faintly and gave them the only answer I could: "They're working on it."

My father, who had been anxiously awaiting my return to India, often reminded me of my age and gently asked if I was ready to settle down and get married. Given my circumstances, I didn't feel prepared to commit to anything, not until I found a decent job. Still, I didn't want to disappoint him, so I said, "Yes, I'm thinking about it. But do you know someone who's a good match and ready for marriage?"

Perhaps anticipating my answer, my father, who had arranged marriages for seven of my elder siblings and many others in the community, responded without hesitation. He told me he'd already received proposals from the parents of several well-educated girls, including one with a Ph.D. If I agreed, he said, he could arrange for me to meet them the following week.

"No, not that soon," I interrupted. "Let me think about it first."

"Okay, whatever you say," he replied.

I could tell from his body language he wasn't pleased with my answer.

Returning to India was not the homecoming I had imagined. My arrival at the Amritsar International Airport in June 1982 turned into a lengthy ordeal. Customs officials spent hours inspecting my luggage before slapping a 320% duty on an electric Olivetti typewriter, arguing it was an electronic device and arbitrarily inflating its value. They disregarded the official receipts I had from a New York shop and refused to verify the price over a phone call. Amritsar's airport was still small and underdeveloped, with no facilities for visitors. So the twenty-plus relatives who came to receive me were forced to wait for hours in the blistering heat, with temperatures soaring past 100°F. I saw no point in paying such a steep duty, so I left the typewriter behind.

Although it was heartwarming to reunite with family and friends after nearly five years, I soon found the atmosphere stifling. Everyone I met seemed to want to know every detail of my life. Conversations revolved around money, possessions, and comparisons. People boasted about their wealth, asked how much I had earned in Canada, and speculated how much I had brought with me. The focus on financial success was overwhelming.

Even my elder brother remarked, "After all those years of education, you still don't have a good job? Do you really think it's worth it? I doubt your future salary will match what my sons, half your age and with only high school diplomas, are earning daily. If you like, I'll hire you as a manager at one of my stores, you'll make more than any other job can offer."

At home, the pressure to get married and settle down continued, despite my ongoing job search and financial uncertainty. I felt boxed in, burdened by expectations I wasn't ready to meet. To escape it all, I considered returning to the United States. Any job would do, just to find some space, less scrutiny, fewer questions, and certainly less pressure to marry immediately.

Until that moment, I had never imagined that my move to India, what I had once considered permanent, would end up being so brief.

But then came the big question, how would I get a visa to enter the U.S.? For someone my age, it was a difficult process, but this time, I got lucky. Just as I was finishing my studies in Canada and actively looking for a job, a scientist involved in organizing a week-long annual conference on Plant Pathology in Salt Lake City, Utah, invited me to attend. The conference was scheduled for August 1982, and his reasoning made sense: since most Postdoc and Research Associate positions were advertised locally rather than in national publications, attending the event might help me meet someone in person who could offer me a job.

When I later reached out to the organizers, they quickly agreed to send me a formal invitation. It felt like good timing. Even if nothing else came of it, the invitation alone could help me obtain a U.S. visa. And it did. Once I had all the documents, the staff at the U.S. Consular Office in New Delhi issued the visa without delay and wished me well on my journey.

The only problem was the tight schedule. The conference was to begin in just a week, leaving me only four or five days to arrange everything. That included converting my Canadian bank draft into Indian rupees quickly so I could buy an airline ticket before flights filled up, traveling back to my village to pack, inventing a story to tell my parents so they wouldn't worry, and catching a connecting flight to Salt Lake City after clearing U.S. immigration in New York.

Traveling after the conference had already started could have jeopardized my entry. Fortunately, my younger brother stepped in and made everything possible. He arranged for my Canadian dollars to be converted swiftly and helped with other preparations. Thanks to his support, I made it to the airport and boarded my flight to New York on time.

The flight had a brief stopover in London. From there, I called Mr. Singh, my longtime friend who had moved to Detroit, to inform him of my travel plans and let him know I'd follow up once I landed in New York. I arrived at JFK well past midnight. Before taking the connecting flight to Detroit, I called Singh again and asked him to pick me up from the airport later that day.

The immigration officials had granted me a six-month stay, so I decided to spend a few days with Singh before making any other plans. He met me at the airport as promised.

The next morning, anxious about finding a job, I skipped rest and set out right after a light breakfast. I started walking along Woodward Avenue, one of Detroit's busiest roads stretching over 20 miles from downtown to Pontiac. I walked nearly seven miles in one direction and the same distance back, knocking on doors of every business that was open. I wasn't picky, I asked for any job: dishwasher, busboy, cashier, anything that would allow me to cover my own basic needs without having to borrow from Singh.

But no one would hire me. Some required prior experience, even for entry-level roles, and others asked for documentation like a work permit or a Social Security number, neither of which I could show at the time. Still, I didn't give up.

The following day, I visited Wayne State University to meet Dr. Hari, a research scientist I had been referred to earlier by his senior collegue Dr. Seigal. To my great luck, he had an opening for a Postdoctoral Research Fellow and offered me the position, pending approval of my work permit. Thankfully, the university took care of all the paperwork and fees, and within a week, I had my H-1B status approved.

Singh and I were overjoyed. That same evening, we hosted a small celebration, inviting his friends from the area. As usual, after a few shots of Johney Whiskey, Singh began teasing me again, bringing up how foolish I had been to leave the U.S. for India in the first place and waste time and money in the process. I thought he had a point, but I stayed quiet. At that moment, getting my first job offer in the United States felt far more important than arguing about what could've been.

"Counting Plates after the Dinner! What's the Point?"

Before leaving Canada, I reached out to my close friend Singh, who by that time had settled in Detroit, Michigan. When I told him about my plans to return to India, after a brief stopover at JFK airport in New York, he suggested I extend the stop and spend a week with him before heading back. I had never visited New York during all my years in Canada, and knowing it might be a long time before we'd see each other again, I accepted his offer.

During our time in New York, Singh reminded me that being in the United States was a rare opportunity and urged me to reconsider my decision to return to India without first securing a permanent residency, a green card. But I was resolute. My decision was rooted in two firm reasons: I had signed a bond with the Government of India requiring my return after studies, and more personally, my mother had been unwell and longed for my return. I told Singh, "Now I must go. But, God willing, I might come back."

After a memorable week together, I left for India from JFK.

Roughly two and a half months later, I was back at the same airport. This time, my destination was Detroit, Michigan, where I planned to stay as long as my U.S. visa allowed. It was nearing midnight when I called Singh. I told him I was flying in and asked if he could pick me up a few hours later. He was stunned. "You were so adamant about going back.

Why now? Why spend all that money just to return in a few weeks? If you were going to come back, you could've stayed in India longer."

I replied simply, "I'll explain when I get there."

Around 4 a.m., Singh met me at the Detroit airport. He was living in a rented basement of a three-story colonial house near Eight Mile Road in Detroit. The landlady, an elderly woman in her late seventies or early eighties, occupied the upper two floors. She lived alone and, rather than renting out the basement for profit, preferred having someone there for safety and company. Her rent was modest, and she had few concerns, only that the noise stayed down and utility bills were fairly shared.

The basement was well-equipped: a full bathroom, a decent-sized kitchen, a storage room, an exercise area, and a spacious multipurpose room. There was enough space for two twin beds, a sofa, a coffee table, a television area, and additional storage or even another bed. My arrival didn't trouble her; on the contrary, she welcomed me warmly and offered every kindness to make my stay comfortable.

Singh treated me like family. He shared his space generously, showed me around the area, guided me on job hunting, and even let me use his car freely. Thankfully, my Manitoba driver's license was valid in Michigan, at least until I secured a local one.

After I secured a job at Wayne State University, my attention naturally shifted to finding a life partner. As for where I'd live, that had already been decided for me. My friend had said firmly, "Until you get married, don't even think about moving." So I stayed put, our place was only five or six miles from work, and it made sense for the time being.

The house had just one bathroom in the basement, so we had to establish a morning routine to keep things smooth and punctual. The rule was simple: whoever got up first used the bathroom; the other cleaned the dishes left over from the night before, and took meat out of the freezer to thaw for dinner. I usually woke up earlier, so I'd claim the bathroom first. The arrangement worked well, especially on weekdays. Weekends were more relaxed. Saturday nights, we either hosted a gathering or went out and came back late, so our little system had some wiggle room.

Singh, my roommate, loved celebrating, especially with a few drinks. Weekends or special occasions, any excuse would do. One day, his auntie from Canada called to say she and her family would visit the following Sunday. They would stay a couple of hours before heading back, an eight-hour round trip, she reminded him, since they all had work the next day. Singh had been urging her to visit for a long time. He respected her deeply, treated her like a mother, so the news thrilled him. He was determined to make their short stay memorable.

By the time Sunday arrived, Singh had everything set: their favorite food, plenty of drinks, and dinner already cooked. As soon as his guests arrived, he and his uncle wasted no time cracking open a bottle of whisky. The snacks were already laid out. Laughter and conversation flowed freely, and the drinks kept coming. But after a while, his auntie began hinting that it was getting late. She asked Singh if dinner was ready or if they should just head home since the snacks had filled them up anyway. Singh, however, seemed not to hear her, or perhaps he simply ignored the suggestion and kept pouring drinks, caught up in the moment.

His auntie glanced at me, perhaps hoping I might know what was going on. Realizing they were on the verge of leaving, and that I had work early the next morning, I stood up, reheated the steaks Singh had prepared, and served them with the side dishes. After dinner, the guests left promptly. Singh, half-asleep by then, started snoring soon after they walked out the door. I rinsed the dishes, left them in the sink, and went to bed.

Monday morning, routine resumed. I got up early and went to the bathroom. Singh woke up soon after and headed to the kitchen. When I finished and went to check on him, I was surprised to see he hadn't touched the dishes yet. Instead, he was standing over the sink, staring down.

"What's going on?" I asked.

He didn't answer, just gestured for me to wait and kept counting the plates.

"Counting plates? After dinner? What's the point?"

He said nothing, just started recounting.

Back in India, I'd seen caterers count plates after events to calculate costs, but we were in the U.S., and last night's guests were close family. I couldn't make sense of it. Was he still drunk? Hungover? But no, he was alert, talking normally, not stumbling or slurring. Why waste precious time in the morning when he needed to be getting ready for work?

Maybe he thought a plate had broken? But if so, he would've tossed the pieces and moved on. My curiosity was piqued, so I lingered.

Finally, Singh paused, looked at me, and said, "I'm trying to figure out whether I ate dinner last night."

I blinked. "What?"

"If there's one plate fewer than the number of people here last night, it means I didn't eat. And if I didn't eat, it means I was probably too drunk. Which means I may have said something stupid to them. In that case, I'll need to call and apologize." I stared at him, stunned. "Sorry," I said, half-laughing, half-bewildered. "You've got a big project in hand, and I can't help you with that."

I grabbed my bag and left for work, still shaking my head as I stepped outside.

Finding My Life Partner

In 1981, as I turned 31, my highest priority was to complete the requirements for my Ph.D. It was the final year my scholarship was approved, and according to the rules of the Government of India, any extension beyond that required a formal application explaining why more time was needed, without any guarantee it would be granted. So, understandably, finding a life partner was the last thing on my mind.

To my surprise, however, a family from a rural town near Winnipeg, Manitoba, whom I had visited once for a winter picnic, approached me with a marriage proposal. They belonged to a Punjabi Jat community, rooted in farming villages across Punjab. One of their daughters, a woman in her late twenties, was studying dentistry at the same university as me. As she was also unmarried, her parents wished to explore the possibility of a match, provided both sides felt comfortable.

Although I wasn't seeking any new commitment beyond finishing my degree, I considered their proposal. I had already met the young woman during my earlier visit and had found her to be kind and of good character. Given my age and the respectful nature of the approach, I agreed to let the family look into my background if they wished.

Soon after, they reached out to their relatives in India, asking them to visit my parents and verify various details, one of which was how much land my parents owned. In farming communities, land ownership can often be a make-or-break factor in marriage discussions, being viewed as a measure of both stability and status.

My father, however, had a very different mindset. After fleeing what became Pakistan during the Partition in 1947, he left everything behind, land, business, and savings, to ensure his family's survival. Since then, he hadn't owned any property except for a modest home they were renting and later bought, with some financial help I had sent while studying in Canada.

When asked about the family's landholdings, my father didn't respond with figures. Instead, he posed a question: "How much land does a person really need?" The relatives were puzzled. "What do you mean?" they asked.

He explained calmly, "When someone dies, all they need is about three and a half square yards to be buried or cremated. I have enough land for that."

Shocked, the relatives left without further discussion. When my father recounted the story to me later, I couldn't help but smile and commend him. "They got a fitting reply," I said, "They failed to see the value of education that we were both striving for, and instead were fixated on land that's thousands of miles away."

I never heard from the girl's family again, and I never felt the need to contact them either.

After completing my degree, I returned to India. No sooner had I arrived than my parents reminded me that I was already

32 and asked when I planned to "settle down." In Canada, that kind of question usually surfaces when someone turns eighteen, finishes high school, and parents want to know when their child will get a job and move out. But in India, the phrase has an entirely different meaning, it's about marriage and starting a family, not moving out. In fact, except for daughters who traditionally move in with their in-laws after marriage, parents in India often feel abandoned if their sons leave the family home, whether married or not.

Sensing what they really meant, I asked my father lightly, "Why? Do you have someone in mind?"

He answered without missing a beat. "Actually, I know of three girls, all from good families and well educated. One of them even has a Ph.D. They're willing to come meet us next week, if that's okay with you."

His quick response caught me off guard. "No, not that fast," I said. "I need to find a job first. Otherwise, both I and my future partner would be financially dependent on you. I'm working on it and hope to find something suitable soon."

"Okay, as you wish," he replied, though his tone made it clear he wasn't entirely pleased.

In the following two months, although I struggled to find a suitable job, I received exciting news: an invitation to attend a scientific conference in the United States. After having lived in Canada for four and a half years, I had changed significantly. Not having a job and depending on my parents felt uncomfortable and unacceptable. I found myself unfit for a system that rarely worked for people like me, those without connections or political leverage. So, I began exploring job opportunities elsewhere, primarily in Canada and the United States.

The conference invitation felt like a windfall. Thankfully, I had saved enough money during my time in Canada, so finances weren't an issue. Still, the question that lingered in my mind was, "Will this plan work?" It wasn't the first time I had gambled with my savings. "Why not take another chance? After all, what other options do I have?" I reasoned. The more I thought about it, the clearer it became that I had to give it a shot.

I also recalled from my previous experiences that most post-doctoral fellowship positions in Canada or the U.S. were advertised at conference sites, and rarely anywhere else. My main concern, however, was the money I had saved in Canada. It was in the form of a bank draft in Canadian dollars, which would take weeks, if not months, to convert into Indian currency, necessary for purchasing things like air tickets. This was where my younger brother's connections came in handy. Within a week, I was on my way to the conference, hopeful that I would meet as many subject matter experts as possible and, with a little luck, land a job.

"If it doesn't work out, if I don't find a job right away, I'll apply for another Ph.D. or MD program to extend my legal stay and keep trying," I thought. I felt good about having a backup plan. Sitting in the plane enroute to New York, I realized that having a plan was the best decision I had made.

The thought reminded me of the saying, "People don't plan to fail, but fail to plan."

Before I left home, I told my parents that I had found a job in Hyderabad, a large city in Southern India, and needed to move there soon, "like tomorrow." I said this to avoid giving them too much of a shock. My plan to attend the conference worked. I landed a job offer to work at Wayne State University in Detroit, Michigan. A close friend of mine, Singh, who had lived and studied with me for years, was also in Detroit. He assured me I could stay with him for as long as I needed. He was renting a basement room from an elderly woman who lived upstairs, and he didn't mind sharing it with me. I gladly accepted his offer.

Having secured a job and a place to live brought me immense relief. It felt as though I had won the gamble I had taken. However, it wasn't long before I was engulfed by new concerns. The job offer had helped me secure a work permit for at least three years, with the possibility of extending it for another three years, provided my employer petitioned for it. This was a huge relief, but I couldn't shake the thought: what if my boss, the petitioner, changed his mind or lost the grant that supported my employment? If I couldn't find an alternative, I'd have no choice but to return to India, which I had no desire to do at that time. This was one of my two major concerns; the other was the pressure I felt from my parents, who considered me to be getting "old" by Indian standards.

Singh and I discussed the issue and concluded that the only permanent solution would be to find a life partner already living in the U.S. and get married. This would grant me Permanent Resident status (a Green Card), which seemed like the best resolution to both of my concerns. I must admit, at that time, I didn't realize that I could apply for a Green Card through my employment status. Even if I had known, pursuing that route would have taken many years, especially to find a suitable partner whom my parents approved of. Thus, marrying someone who was already in the U.S. with a Green Card seemed to offer the quickest solution. So, my search for a life partner became more urgent.

As I began looking for a life partner, I soon realized that it was one of the hardest challenges I had ever faced. While my job as a post-doctoral research fellow was demanding, I still had to find time to focus on this personal quest. I was smart enough when it came to grades, scholarships, and technical work, but I was socially awkward. As always, Singh came to my rescue, providing much-needed guidance, support, and rides to wherever we needed to go. He took me to clubs, bars, and beaches, places where I might meet single women. He even made calls on my behalf to arrange dates with interested girls, as he noticed my social and communication skills were lacking.

We perused newspaper ads, made inquiries with friends and relatives, and traveled near and far, hoping to meet the right person. We did meet some women and their families along the way, but there was always something that didn't work out, and we'd end up back at square one, frustrated and arguing. I remember one particular ad in a vernacular newspaper from a girl's parents in Houston, TX. The girl's background seemed to match everything I was looking for, so I called her parents, and after speaking with them, I learned that we had a lot in common, both from similar backgrounds in India and both speaking Punjabi and Hindi at home. I flew to Houston to meet them the following weekend. But again, something didn't work out, and the girl and her parents wouldn't discuss the issue. Needless to say, Singh and I were both very disappointed.

A few weeks later, I came across another ad in the newspaper, this time for a girl in Silver Spring, MD. Her background was almost identical to the girl from Houston, so I expressed my interest in visiting her family. The family, her mother, brother, sister-in-law, and two kids, welcomed me. Upon meeting the girl and her relatives, I conveyed my intention to marry her, provided they felt the same. After conducting their due diligence, including having their relatives meet my parents in India, the girl, Kusam, and her family gave their affirmative decision. The process moved quickly, and by May 1983, we were married in a religious ceremony at a Gurdwara in Silver Spring, MD. A month later, we went through the legal process in a court in Ferndale, MI.

The day before our scheduled social wedding, in compliance with my father's rule of keeping the groom's party (Baraat) small, no more than five or eleven people, I took a total of five people, including myself, in a car. We were received by close to 250 people on Kusam's side at her residence in Silver Spring. The following day, we were married in the local Gurdwara.

My groom party with Kusam at the engagement ceremony

Wedding ceremony at a Gurdwara in Silver Spring, MD in 1983 -1

Wedding ceremony at a Gurdwara in Silver Spring, MD in 1983 -2

Everyone who knew me, whether in India or the U.S., was stunned to hear the news of our marriage, to the point of disbelief. My younger brother wrote to me immediately, bombarding me with questions. He wanted to know everything about Kusam Gadh, now his sister-in-law, about the wedding process, and, most of all, about the urgency that led to our marriage happening so quickly.

I remember answering his questions about Kusam by using an analogy, comparing her to a cricketer who scores six runs on six attempts. I explained, "She is six years younger than me, six inches shorter, six grades less educated, and lives near Washington D.C., which is about six hundred miles away from where I live. We got married in 1983, exactly six years after I first left India in 1977, and interestingly, we were legally married in June, the sixth month of the year. So, in every way you can think of, I scored sixes."

Visiting my folks in India after marriage. The house is same as I had lived in during my school days but got remodeled just prior to our visit in 1986.

Four years later, in 1987, we were blessed with a beautiful girl. From the moment she was born, she became everything to us, daughter, son, friend, and a constant source of up-to-date information. She has always been someone we are immensely proud of.

In 2020, she proved to be a lifesaver when I suffered a severe nerve attack. The attack left me completely paralyzed, unable to move my limbs or speak a single word. I was in the intensive care unit for weeks, breathing through a ventilator and fighting for my life. During that time, she communicated with my healthcare providers using video charts and made sure my medical needs were met, including administering insulin. Perhaps she was a God-sent angel, fulfilling this critical role. Despite the gravity of the situation, she made it a priority to care for her mother, Kusam, even if it meant taking significant time off from her work.

"It's Me, Bobby, Mama Ji!"

After completing my Ph.D. studies in Canada in 1982, I conducted an extensive search for employment opportunities in Canada, India, and the United States. My efforts finally paid off when I received a job offer as a Postdoctoral Research Fellow at Wayne State University (WSU) in Detroit, Michigan. The job involved researching the molecular biology of plant viruses, specifically determining the replication site of the tobacco etch virus in infected tobacco leaf cells. Although my salary was much lower than the standard pay for U.S. citizens or permanent residents newly hired as postdocs, I was happy to have a professional job instead of working at an entry-level position in retail. The job was interesting, and it also provided me with a legal permit to work in the United States.

While employed at WSU, I realized I was already 32 years old, and it was time to settle down. Another concern was not wanting to rely on the University for my stay in the U.S. So, I began looking for a life partner, someone who could also help me secure permanent resident status. It didn't take long, and within a year, I was married to a Punjabi woman who lived not far from me, in the outskirts of Washington, D.C. As planned, just a week before the wedding, I rented a one-bedroom apartment near the university and moved there. My wife joined me after the wedding. Although the apartment was heavily infested with cockroaches, she had no issue living there, understanding that with our limited income, we couldn't afford anything better near the university.

Two years passed, and my wife, who was desperately seeking a day job, was still unemployed. She had good typing skills but lacked the speed required to land an office job. After she completed some training in computerized word processing, we decided to start a typing business from home. Within a couple of months, the business picked up and started generating a decent income. Every day, she would type, and I would proofread the documents at night, after my lab work was done, often working past midnight until the job was completed.

Then one day, while I was working in the lab, I received a surprise phone call. A lady who identified herself as a telephone operator asked if I was willing to accept a collect call. I agreed, and before she could finish, I heard someone shouting in Punjabi in the background, "It's me, Bobby, Mama ji, please accept." It was my nephew, Bobby, who was 25 years old. He had called collect from an airport in Texas to inform me of his arrival there a few hours earlier. He was on his way to visit us in the United States after a stopover in Guatemala. Although he was vague on details, he sounded confident. At my suggestion, Bobby continued calling me collect from Guatemala over the next few days to keep me updated on his travel plans.

A day or two later, Bobby called again from a motel in Guatemala. He told me that his travel agent, who had assisted him and others in reaching Guatemala, had gone to Nicaragua to get U.S. visas for everyone. Bobby mentioned that he would be back soon to take Bobby and his companions to the U.S. without much hassle. As usual, Bobby was evasive with details and didn't allow me to ask many questions. He sounded hurried, as though someone else needed the public phone, or perhaps he was aware of how costly the long collect calls were.

After that call, I looked at the world map and saw that Guatemala and Nicaragua were far apart, each with its own U.S. consulate to issue visas. So, I couldn't understand why the agent had to go to Nicaragua. Bobby's statement didn't make sense to me. I raised serious doubts about the agent's plan, citing some media reports, and suggested to Bobby and his friends that they should look for alternative ways to leave that place. Those doubts soon proved to be true. A couple of days later, Bobby called again to inform me that the agent had disappeared. A local contact was now working with the agent's friends in the U.S. and that they would need some money to cover the expenses. Bobby assured me they would be in the U.S. "pretty soon." He didn't offer any more details, probably because much of the communication was in Spanish, which neither he nor his Punjabi friends could understand.

Three days later, I received another call from Bobby. This time, he told me that he and his friends had crossed into the U.S. through the Texas-Mexico border, only to be caught by U.S. authorities when they tried to board a plane to other destinations in the country. Now, he was calling from a detention center. During our subsequent calls, Bobby explained that while crossing the border, he had lost his "Mehar" (a saffron-colored cloth given to him by a holy saint before he left India), which he considered a blessing. He was very worried about being deported and pleaded for me to do

144

something quickly to get him out of the detention center. His voice sounded as if he were crying.

I had no experience dealing with situations like this. All I could say was, "OK, let me see what I can do." Financially, I was barely making ends meet, with no savings to pay for an agent or attorney, the bail amount, or travel expenses, these costs ran into the thousands of dollars. My own application for permanent resident status was still pending, which kept me from taking any risks by visiting him in the detention center. So, I had no choice but to involve my best friend, Singh.

Singh did an excellent job. He found an attorney and arranged all the necessary payments immediately. The attorney made several representations to a local judge in Texas over the next 2-3 weeks, ultimately getting Bobby's bail reduced and securing his release. Singh and the attorney then made arrangements for Bobby to be flown to Detroit, where we would pick him up. Although we had heard that Bobby wasn't feeling well in detention, the shock came when we saw him at the airport. He looked very skinny, was in a wheelchair, and needed assistance from the airline staff. Not only did Bobby look too weak to move on his own, but he also resisted sitting in Singh's car, superstitiously fearing that something bad would happen to us if he did.

Bobby seemed to have lost a lot of weight. He looked like a 10- to 12-year-old boy, weighing less than 80 lbs. Although we had heard from Bobby's attorney that he hadn't been eating properly in the detention center and had become very weak because of it, seeing him in such poor condition was a complete shock. Singh and I had to physically lift him from the wheelchair and into the car, urging him to hurry so we could move the car from the arrivals platform. We promised him we would address his questions and concerns once we were out of the airport.

Once we got home, Bobby's resistance to getting out of the car and stepping into the apartment grew stronger. When we asked why, he explained that, according to his dreams, one of us, either Kusam or I, would not survive if he ever entered our home. He kept repeating that he had lost his "blessings" and that his friends had made him cut his hair to cross the border with them. We realized that Bobby was mentally disturbed, which helped us understand why the detention authorities and judge had quickly agreed to reduce his bail.

Singh and I once again helped him out of the car and forced him into the apartment, where my wife was anxiously waiting. It was already past 10 pm. Within minutes, another friend who had heard about Bobby's arrival from Kusam stopped by. We listened to Bobby talk non-stop about his lost blessings, his hair, and how one of us would die. Singh, my friend, and I all agreed that Bobby's weak physical and mental condition could be the result of a lack of proper food and sleep in the detention center, so we tried to feed him and get him to sleep as soon as possible.

We also decided to have a specialist assess him, so I called a friend who was training to become a certified psychiatrist. I explained the situation, and he understood the gravity of it, deciding to come over that same night. He brought prescriptions with him, based on our conversation, and told us that Bobby needed good sleep within the next two or three days, or else he risked permanent nerve damage. After a quick dinner, all our friends left.

For the next two nights, we continued giving Bobby the prescribed medicine, but despite that, he kept talking and crying without falling asleep. My wife and I took turns holding him tight, making him lie between us on the bed. We stayed awake for most of those nights, terrified that his condition might become permanent.

Then, on the third night, something changed. Bobby finally fell asleep soundly, and so did we. I noticed that one of the windows facing the street had been left wide open overnight, causing some noise. The next morning, we were astonished to see Bobby acting completely normal, even apologizing for all the trouble he had caused since his arrival. Was it the medication finally taking effect, the noise outside that helped him sleep, or a combination of both? We weren't sure. What mattered was that we were all finally able to sleep soundly again. It felt like a miracle, and we all thanked God.

Over the next year, Bobby managed to get his driver's license and eventually decided to move to California after a promise from a distant relative, a business owner, who assured him of a job. A few months later, Bobby switched jobs to work for a convenience store chain located about 60 miles east of Los Angeles.

Business vs Job, What's Better?

Four years after joining Wayne State University (WSU), my employer informed me that unless the grant funding my position was renewed, my contract would end in a few months. I was advised to start exploring other opportunities. As luck would have it, I ended up moving to East Lansing, MI, in 1986 to work for Michigan State University. It was here that we were blessed with a baby girl.

To help us out, we asked both my mother-in-law and father to come stay with us. Expecting as much, they both gladly agreed, promising to stay for as long as we needed them. With both sets of parents living with us, our monthly expenses increased, and we found ourselves needing a larger place to live. We began looking for additional sources of income.

Recognizing the financial strain, my wife decided to take a part-time job that would allow her to balance work and taking care of the baby. Unfortunately, East Lansing, being a small town, offered few opportunities, and she couldn't find the right fit. We then began to entertain the idea of starting our own business.

After moving from Detroit to East Lansing, my friend Singh, who had often mentioned to me the benefits of owning a business, repeated his suggestion: "Why not start a business together?" He spoke about the freedom of being your own boss, avoiding the uncertainty of switching jobs, and the stability that ownership could provide. However, beyond these mentions, no concrete plans had materialized, and we were too preoccupied with the day-to-day challenges of our new life.

Meanwhile, Bobby, my nephew, who had moved to California, was also ready for a change. He was tired of being alone and wanted to come back to Michigan. Having gained some experience working at a convenience store, Bobby proposed that we start a business together. Ever since arriving in the US, he had been eager to begin this venture. "Why not do some business together?" he often asked. His offer to return home provided the support I needed, giving me the assurance that our family would back the decision. The only question left was what kind of business we could start that would require minimal capital and where we would find that capital.

Just then, as if some higher power was listening, Singh brought us a newspaper advertisement. A franchisor, Dairy Mart, was offering an opportunity to own a convenience store franchise with a relatively low startup cost. The catch was that I would need to resign from my professional job and move back to Detroit, where this business opportunity existed.

We reviewed the details and agreed that it was a unique chance to own a business. We also realized that this could bring Singh and us closer again, allowing Bobby, Kusam, and me to work and live together, strengthening our bonds. If everything went well, it might even help us fulfill our American dreams. Seeing it as a win-win situation, I readily agreed to the opportunity.

Within a couple of months and after securing enough financial help from friends and relatives, I resigned from my job and, in partnership with Bobby, opened our own convenience store franchise in a suburb of Detroit. However, just three months after the business launched, the partnership fell apart. The store didn't generate the income we had expected based on the information provided by the franchisor. Bobby, dissatisfied with what he was making, decided to quit and move back to California.

Meanwhile, the franchisor, noticing my good performance and responding to my repeated requests for a busier store that would provide higher income, eventually offered both Bobby and me separate stores at different locations. Over the next three years of running the business, the franchisor grew dissatisfied with our performance. After discovering that I had started a computer-related business on the side with some friends, Dairy Mart decided to take back both stores, mine and Bobby's.

With the computer business still in its infancy, not generating income beyond covering basic maintenance costs, I had no choice but to end the partnership. I then moved to New Jersey, where I decided to start an independent convenience store. The store in New Jersey provided enough income for my wife to sustain herself, but it wasn't enough to cover both of our expenses. This forced me to look for other opportunities.

As luck would have it, I had become a U.S. citizen by this point, which made me eligible for federal jobs. I applied for one and was selected as a Plant Protection and Quarantine

Officer with the U.S. Department of Agriculture. Not only did I get the job, but I also managed to land it without even having to go through an interview. The job involved working as an inspector at airports and seaports in New Jersey, and my education and experience with plant pests were enough to secure the position.

With the salary from this job, I felt that the journey to break free from the vicious cycle had finally begun. We kept the store for a few more years, mainly so my wife had something to occupy her time while I worked long hours. It also ensured that she didn't have to depend on me for petty cash. We eventually sold the business once we realized that my salary alone was enough to support us, and my daughter needed more of her mom's time for schoolwork and extracurricular activities.

So, what's better, owning an independent business or working for someone else? My conclusion is that it depends on a variety of factors, such as your legal status in the U.S., your potential to secure a job based on your education and experience, the capital you can invest in a business, and the support you have from your family.

In our case, while the business provided a good job for my wife, who preferred to be her own boss, it didn't work for us beyond offering a tax shelter for several years, especially once my salary from the federal job grew significantly. In later years, as we shifted to a shipping and mailing business, the combination of my work with the federal government and my wife running the shipping business proved to be very successful. In 2016, the business reached new heights when

I retired from my federal job and joined the business full-time.

In conclusion, whether you run a business or work for someone else, your education and experience play a crucial role in achieving success. In today's fast-paced world, no matter what path you choose, education and technological know-how are indispensable unless you have someone you trust to rely on when needed.

My Wonderful Career at USDA APHIS

About a year after launching our convenience store business in New Jersey, and now officially a U.S. citizen, I began searching for an opportunity to work with the federal government. That long-held dream finally came true when I was offered a position as a Plant Protection and Quarantine Officer with the Animal and Plant Health Inspection Service (APHIS), one of the agencies under the U.S. Department of Agriculture (USDA). APHIS regulates the importation of agricultural goods into the United States, ensuring that invasive pests don't threaten domestic crops and ecosystems.

To my surprise, I was selected for the role without even being interviewed, a rarity, as I later discovered through conversations with my colleagues. They speculated that it may have been due to my academic background, extensive experience with plant pests, and comfort with computer systems. Whatever the reason, it felt like another turning point, one that affirmed years of persistence and preparation.

The only drawback was the job's location: nearly 70 miles from our new home in Burlington Township, New Jersey. The commute was grueling, often involving long workdays that required not just travel to and from the inspection site, but also additional field visits and late-night overtime shifts. On some days, I drove up to 300 miles before finally calling it a day. Still, the job offered excellent pay, generous benefits, and for the first time in my life, a stable and prestigious professional standing. With my wife's resolve to run the store on her own, I accepted the position and began on short notice.

The role turned out to be more than just a job, it was a breakthrough. With overtime included, my income increased significantly. More than that, the position allowed me to put many of my skills to use: math, physics, computers, and critical thinking. One particular challenge stands out from my early days on the job.

APHIS regulations required the fumigation of certain agricultural products at the port of entry, using a chemical gas to eliminate potential pests. The amount of gas needed had to be calculated carefully. Too much, and it could damage the produce or leave unsafe residues; too little, and the pests might survive. The required dosage depended on the volume of the shipment, which in turn depended on the dimensions of the containers being fumigated.

I noticed a flaw in the way volumes were being calculated when a 40-foot and a 20-foot marine container were fumigated together under a shared tarp. The space formed by the tarp overhanging the smaller container created an empty cone, one that was rarely measured accurately. This often resulted in the use of more gas than necessary, just to ensure pest elimination. Drawing on my background in physics and geometry, I developed a formula to more precisely calculate the true volume, including that awkward cone-shaped space.

The outcome was twofold: fumigators used less gas, saving money for importers, and the treatment process became safer for consumers. Eventually, my method was adopted as

154

standard procedure across the site. It was a small change in numbers, but a big shift in practice, and one of the most satisfying accomplishments of my early government career.

Over the years, I rose through the ranks and eventually became an Import Specialist, a management-level position within APHIS. This promotion brought me to the agency's headquarters in the Washington, D.C. area, where I was tasked with overseeing issues related to the importation of agricultural goods from all countries in Asia and Africa.

One of the most challenging and politically sensitive matters on my desk involved mangoes, particularly from India and Pakistan. These countries, major producers of mangoes, had long been eager to gain access to the U.S. market. However, a ban had been in place for over 18 years due to the lack of an approved treatment capable of mitigating the risks posed by pests often found within the fruit. In retaliation, both India and Pakistan had banned certain U.S. exports from entering their markets. The issue had become so entrenched that my supervisor once commented she didn't expect to see a resolution, or a single mango shipment from those countries, during her entire career at APHIS.

China, Thailand, and several other Asian nations had similar unresolved trade barriers and pest risk challenges. Their markets, too important to overlook, were eventually added to my portfolio, expanding both the responsibility and complexity of my role.

One of the most rewarding aspects of the job was the opportunity to travel, representing the United States in discussions around plant health standards, quarantine protocols, and trade negotiations. I found myself navigating conference rooms and field sites alike, sometimes presenting U.S. regulations governing the importation of foreign produce, other times explaining treatment options such as irradiation to mitigate pest risks. In other instances, I worked to support the export of U.S. commodities, like logs, into foreign markets.

My work took me to countries such as Brazil, Canada, China, England, Ethiopia, Germany, India, Japan, Mexico, the Philippines, South Africa, South Korea, and Thailand, among others. Within the U.S., I traveled extensively across dozens of states, as well as Canadian provinces, participating in bilateral negotiations, quarantine evaluations, and technical discussions on both national and international stages.

Table Mountain in Cape Town, South Africa

On top of Table Mountain in Cape Town, South Africa

Supervising log fumigation on ship docked at Japan port -1

Supervising log fumigation on ship docked at Japan port -2

US Embassy officials in Berlin Germany visiting USDA
Booth at Fruit Logistica in Berlin

Fruit Display at Fruit Logistica Festival in Germany, 2004

Meeting with Thai officials on use of irradiation to treat Thai commodities November 2006

Meeting with India Authorities on mango irradiation program November 2006

Visiting and meeting the staff working at the irradiation treatment facility in India in 2006

An irradiation treatment facility in Nasik, Maharashtra, India

In addition to the countries I visited on official business for the United States, I was once honored to represent the United Nations in the Philippines. During that mission, I had the privilege of training the country's plant protection officials on the commodity pre-clearance program and the application of irradiation treatment, tools that significantly enhanced the export potential of their agricultural products to the U.S. and other international markets.

Conducting a UNO-sponsored workshop on irradiation as a treatment of mangoes in Philippines

Plant Protection Officials of the Philippines Government participating in the workshop on irradiation in 2007

Visiting a research lab in Quezon City, Philippines in 2007 working on the use of irradiation on plant pests

On another occasion, I had the honor of visiting South Korea as a keynote speaker at the International Conference on Plant Pathology held in Seoul in October 2012. Traditionally, U.S. representatives at such conferences had their travel expenses

162

covered by the federal government. However, in my case, APHIS declined to fund the trip, citing budget constraints, despite the fact that I was invited as a keynote speaker and would be the sole official representative of the United States, among attendees from the United Nations and more than 100 other countries. When I informed the conference organizers of my inability to attend due to lack of funding, they graciously offered to cover all of my travel expenses. Upon learning this, APHIS reversed its decision and formally approved my participation.

My presentation as a keynote speaker in South Korea in October, 2012

Beyond handling official duties, I found great value in learning about the social and cultural customs of the countries I visited. These experiences helped me approach U.S. trade issues with a heightened sense of sensitivity and awareness, allowing me to avoid potential backlash or legal challenges against U.S. regulations. I was fortunate to play a lead role in developing over thirty federal rules that governed the importation of agricultural goods into the United States, none of which were ever challenged in court.

Over time, I was promoted to senior risk manager, entrusted with overseeing pest risks related to new agricultural commodities entering the U.S. and handling regulatory matters tied to phytosanitary treatments. These treatments, approved and mandated by APHIS, were essential to ensure that agricultural trade did not lead to the spread of exotic pests, either within the U.S. or abroad.

During this phase, the field saw significant innovation in pest mitigation strategies. Treatments expanded beyond traditional chemicals like methyl bromide to non-chemical methods such as cold treatment, hot water dips, and on-farm cultural practices like fruit bagging, planting resistant varieties, or using sterile insects to disrupt pest life cycles. It was also a period of major advancement in the use of irradiation, a process that exposes fruits and vegetables to low doses of radiation, effectively neutralizing most insect pests without affecting the produce.

Recognizing its potential, I championed the use of irradiation as a viable treatment for tropical fruits such as mangoes, which had long been banned from entering the U.S. due to pest concerns. The trade imbalance was palpable, as some of these countries, in turn, restricted U.S. exports in retaliation. Building on earlier regulatory groundwork laid by a colleague who had moved to the Department of Homeland Security, I focused my efforts on navigating APHIS's regulatory framework to approve irradiation treatment.

By March 2007, we achieved a groundbreaking milestone: APHIS approved irradiation not only for the first time in the world for phytosanitary purposes but also as a *generic* treatment. This meant that, instead of approving treatments for each specific pest, crop, and country combination, one irradiation protocol could be applied broadly, regardless of the commodity or its origin. The impact was immediate and far-reaching. Even before the rule was finalized, it generated widespread excitement and became a notable agenda item during President George W. Bush's visit to India in 2006.

Since then, the approval of irradiation has unlocked billions of dollars in global trade. Countries that previously faced bans on their exports, particularly tropical fruits like mangoes, mangosteens, lychees, longans, rambutan, dragon fruit, and guava, were now able to access U.S. markets. In return, previously banned U.S. goods were allowed into those countries. The ripple effect extended to other regions as well; for example, Australian mangoes could now be exported to New Zealand using the same treatment.

In recognition of this transformative achievement, my colleagues and I received a prestigious award from the Secretary of Agriculture in 2007. I'll never forget the moment my supervisor congratulated me, saying, "People spend their entire careers dreaming of such a distinguished honor. But when I looked at your records, you've received not one, but two awards from the Secretary of USDA. I don't know how you feel about it, but I can tell you, we at the management level are incredibly proud. Congratulations. We plan to display your certificate prominently in our front window."

I was deeply immersed in every facet of establishing irradiation treatment: revising regulations, updating treatment manuals, presenting at workshops, including several hosted by the United Nations in the Philippines, writing standard operating procedures, drafting talking points for senior officials, and approving ports and facilities in the U.S. to receive irradiated imports. My involvement became so well known that colleagues in my unit began referring to me affectionately as *"Irradiation Gadh"* instead of *Inder Gadh.*

Receiving award from the Secretary of USDA in 2007

Receiving award from the Secretary of USDA in 2007

dy Smith presents Inder Paul Gadh, team leader for the Irradiation and India Mango initiative with Alan Green

Receiving a recognition from head of USDA APHIS

Twenty-four and a half years after joining APHIS, I decided to retire in 2016 due to health reasons. Looking back now, I can say without hesitation that my time with APHIS was deeply rewarding, truly the best years of my professional life.

At the time of my retirement, my wife was running her own independent shipping business, similar to The UPS Store. She welcomed me into the role of store manager, offering me a flexible space to stay engaged and productive. Former colleagues from APHIS would often stop by to ship packages and, with surprise, ask if I was really retired. I'd always respond with a grin, "No, not 'retired,' just 're-tired' to work at the store."

In August 2019, after years of dedication, my wife decided it was time to move on. The store was thriving, and she felt confident it was the right moment to sell. We found a buyer, and with that, both of us stepped fully into retirement—this time, officially.

"I've been taking those every day for the last 29 years"

In September of 1991, I received an unexpected letter congratulating me on being selected as a Plant Protection and Quarantine Officer. It listed the address where I was to report on September 22, 1991, provided I was still interested. The letter came on USDA APHIS PPQ letterhead and was signed by Dick Ericson, the Officer-in-Charge. There had been no prior interview, and this was the first time I had even heard of him.

On the appointed date, I arrived at the office, introduced myself to the staff, and asked to meet the person whose name appeared on the letter. They directed me to a chair and asked me to wait. A few minutes later, a tall Black man, roughly six feet in height and dressed in a white shirt and black pants, came out of his office and greeted me warmly. From his deep voice and slow movements, I guessed he was around sixty years old. His large build and pronounced stomach gave him a weight of at least 250 pounds, perhaps more. I based that estimate on comparison with my sister-in-law who, although slimmer than him, weighed a bit more than 250 herself.

While speaking, he paused often to catch his breath. After briefly explaining the different operations of the Unit, Dick introduced me to his junior staff: first-line supervisors, officers in khaki uniforms, and a few support personnel. He then left me in the care of one of the supervisors, Diane

Jones, who was tasked with providing my orientation and other onboarding details.

Over the next two to three years, I had several opportunities to interact with Mr. Ericson. I came to know him as a kind man with strong communication and public speaking skills. I later learned that he held a master's degree in agriculture, was remarkably punctual, and typically spent his days in meetings with staff, officers, or outside personnel. He rarely left his office unless an event required his presence, such as greeting new employees, accompanying visiting dignitaries, attending important functions, or making necessary trips like going to the restroom.

Without a doubt, he relied heavily on his supervisors to carry out much of the Unit's day-to-day administrative work. It wasn't uncommon to see supervisors going in and out of his office throughout the day, often one after another.

Among staff, there was frequent light-hearted commentary about his physical appearance. Some joked about his socks never matching, black on one foot, blue on the other. Upon observing him more closely, I realized his large stomach might have made it difficult for him to see his own feet. Putting on socks was probably a challenge, let alone choosing matching colors. There was also the matter of timing, he often left for work in the early hours of the morning, before daylight, when it was harder to distinguish between dark shades like black and navy blue.

Another thing I noticed was that his office door was usually shut. Initially, I assumed he was in constant meetings, but I later discovered from coworkers that this wasn't always the case. He had been taking certain medications and, due to his early wake-up schedule and long commute, would sometimes nap in his office. He snored heavily, and out of courtesy and perhaps self-consciousness, he kept the door tightly closed.

As he once confided to me, he was weary of the 70-mile drive each way to and from work, but he didn't have many alternatives.

I personally had no issues with Mr. Ericson during my first two or three years of employment. Most of my interactions were through his first-line supervisors, so I seldom saw him. But whenever we did cross paths, he treated me with respect. He often asked about my computer skills and occasionally sought my help on certain technical matters. At times, he even asked whether I'd be interested in working with the pest identifiers stationed about ten miles northeast of the Unit. "It'll help your chances of promotion," he would say, as if he could read my mind.

When I brought up the idea of driving straight to the pest identifier facility, rather than stopping at the Unit first—he agreed. Since I was already commuting over 70 miles one way, stopping at the Unit would only delay the trip by another hour. He saw the practicality of my suggestion and approved it without hesitation.

Physical fitness was emphasized throughout orientation and new officers' training. The nature of our work, boarding ships and planes, inspecting remote areas, demanded stamina and health. During one of my annual checkups, my doctor noted elevated blood pressure and cholesterol levels. He prescribed medication I would need to take daily. The news was a shock. I was slightly overweight, perhaps by four or five pounds, and while I did feel some pressure from work and side business ventures, I didn't think it would lead to this.

Almost immediately, I experienced side effects. I had to use the restroom more often, possibly due to the amount of water I drank to take the pills. I also began feeling lightheaded at times. That dizziness gave me a new sense of empathy for Mr. Ericson. I now had a small window into how he might feel during the day, especially given his age and physical condition.

I wanted to share this with him, but his schedule was packed and the opportunity never came, until he proposed that we carpool. Since we both lived in southern New Jersey, he suggested we ride together to and from work whenever possible. I welcomed the idea. With nearly 70 miles of highway ahead of us each way, I figured we'd have plenty of time to talk, and perhaps I could finally bring up my situation.

The next morning, he came to work with someone else, but after work, he rode back with me. From that day on, I became his designated driver, which I didn't mind. I had been driving alone anyway, and now I had company. Having someone beside me on the NJ Turnpike after a long day was reassuring, especially given the ever-present risk of drowsiness behind the wheel.

That said, Dick wasn't exactly a chatty co-pilot. He was usually more interested in catching up on sleep than in making conversation. Our exchanges were limited, maybe a few words when getting into the car, another sentence when he stirred mid-ride, and something brief when we arrived. As soon as we hit the highway, he'd fall asleep within minutes. And to say he slept quietly would be inaccurate; his snoring was anything but subtle.

On that first day of carpooling, I was all set to share the shocking news about my health. I figured I'd wait until traffic eased a bit, rush hour had flooded the roads with cars and heavy trucks pouring in from the ports and airports of New Jersey and New York. As usual, the New Jersey Turnpike was packed. That was our standard route home to Willingboro and Burlington Township. Depending on the day, the drive could take anywhere from ninety minutes to two hours, so I wasn't in any particular hurry.

I kept my focus on maneuvering through the congestion as efficiently and safely as possible. Meanwhile, Dick looked entirely unbothered. Either he trusted my driving, or the need to sleep was stronger than his interest in road conditions. Before long, he had drifted off.

As soon as I found my rhythm on the highway, I saw a chance to bring up the subject and maybe get him talking.

"Yesterday I had my annual checkup," I began, glancing over at him. "My doctor checked my vitals and said my blood pressure and cholesterol are still high. He prescribed meds, daily ones, for life, and..."

I didn't get to finish. A quiet snore answered me.

I glanced at him again. He was fast asleep.

Had he heard a word I said? Probably not. If he had, I imagined he would've at least responded.

About thirty minutes later, he stirred and mumbled, "Lots of traffic. You okay?"

"Yeah," I replied, "might be from the Yankee Stadium too. I think the game just ended."

He didn't say anything more, so I figured I'd try again. I repeated the bit about the doctor and the medications. But just like before, he said nothing. I turned to look, he was already asleep again. This time, at least, the snoring wasn't as loud.

Another hour passed, and I finally took the exit off the Turnpike. After clearing the toll booth, I turned onto a slower back road. That's when I noticed he was fully awake again. He looked out the window and then nodded with a bit of appreciation.

"Smart move taking the back road," he said. "How much longer?"

"Ten minutes, at most," I told him.

I didn't want to miss the opportunity again. So, for the third time, I told him about my checkup, the high vitals, and the daily meds. This time, thankfully, he didn't nod off.

Instead, he listened. And then, in a calm, steady voice, said, "Don't worry. I've been taking those every day for the last twenty-nine years."

By then, we'd arrived at his place. He stepped out of the car and added, "We'll talk more about that tomorrow. Have a good one."

"You too," I replied.

As I drove off toward home, I felt an unexpected sense of relief. I couldn't quite explain it, but it felt like a weight had lifted. Maybe it was just the shock of the diagnosis, dulled a little by finally saying it out loud to someone who understood.

Venturing into South Africa, "But No Bungee Jumping Please"

In 1999, as part of APHIS' temporary duty assignment, I had the opportunity to visit Cape Town, South Africa, a city famous for its iconic Table Mountain and often featured in big-budget Bollywood films. My assignment was focused on inspecting citrus fruit destined for the United States. The objective was to ensure that no pests beyond the threshold level were found in small, randomly sampled lots before the fruit underwent Cold Treatment to meet U.S. entry requirements.

For this reason, I was stationed in Stellenbosch, a town about 60 miles east of Cape Town, nestled within the Western Cape province. Stellenbosch was a hub of citrus packaging and shipping industries and was especially known for clementine production. Beyond citrus, the region was world-renowned for its grape cultivation and vineyards, producing some of the finest wines exported across the globe.

Upon my arrival at Cape Town Airport, I was greeted by Michael, a high-ranking official from the South Africa Department of Agriculture. He had come in an official vehicle to drive me to Stellenbosch. As we drove through the picturesque landscape, Michael pointed out the wineries and vineyards that lined the road and asked if I'd be interested in stopping briefly to visit one of the cellars. I agreed.

His English, though not flawless, was clear and understandable. Curious, I asked which language he spoke at home. "Afrikaans," he said. Then, with a playful tone, he asked, "If you don't mind me asking, what type of wine do you prefer to drink?"

I replied honestly, "Believe it or not, I used to enjoy all kinds of wine, beer, and whisky, until last year, when I stopped drinking entirely." Before I could finish my sentence, he cut in, half-laughing, "Then why did you have to come to Stellenbosch of all places? It's the second most important wine-producing town in the world!"

I smiled and offered a brief apology, promising to share the full story behind my decision to quit alcohol another time. We continued on and stopped at a large wine cellar. The place was vast, spanning nearly the size of a football field, and quite impressive in its scale. I mentioned to Michael that my wife, daughter, and my wife's niece would be joining me a few weeks later. I told him they would likely enjoy returning to this place, as all three appreciated wine tasting.

Back on the road, Michael explained my housing options. I could rent an apartment, a condominium, or even share a home, with or without the host family present. However, he had thoughtfully reserved a hotel room for me for one night to help me settle in and decide my next steps. He even offered his own home as an option, inviting me to visit it the next day before making a decision.

The following morning, Michael took me on a tour of the facilities where citrus was processed, packaged, and inspected. He introduced me to a range of people, from officials in the South African government to key stakeholders and technicians who would assist me in the inspection process. Later, he pointed out a few dining options in town, including a popular spot called "Something Fishy," known for its hot, breaded fish and French fries.

After lunch at "Something Fishy" with Michael, I couldn't help but notice a sign inside that read, "Just one bite and you're hooked!" It was a catchy slogan, and I found it to be quite truly. I ended up hooked on that restaurant chain for the rest of my stay.

Michael then took me to his house, where he showed me the front section that I could rent if I decided to stay there. His family of four lived in the back half of the house. It was spacious, with the front area being roughly equivalent to a two-bedroom apartment. Michael and his family were incredibly welcoming, and the house seemed like the ideal environment for my family to settle into while I worked during the weekdays. So, I decided to move in.

When I shared the news with my wife, she was thrilled. She had been concerned about where they would stay when they arrived, so hearing that I had found a good place to stay made her feel much more at ease.

Given that I was assigned for six weeks and had my own rental car, I invited my wife, our 12-year-old daughter, and Mona, my wife's 23-year-old niece, to fly over and join me about three weeks later. Upon their arrival, Michael's family, his wife and two sons, both under 12, welcomed them warmly. The immediate friendliness they received made their stay even more enjoyable than I had expected.

We often shared meals and explored the area together. Our trips included visits to iconic sites such as Table Mountain, the lighthouse marking the southernmost point of the continent, the local wine cellars, a safari, a park with camel rides, and the Cango Caves. Each outing felt like a new adventure, and the time spent with Michael's family made the entire experience richer.

Inside view of the wine cellar

My family along with Michael's visiting the cellar and other places in South Africa

The Light House which is considered the southernmost point
in the continent

Spending an evening with Michael's family and friends in a quiet mountainous place next to Michael's cabin

Family resting on Table Mountain in Cape town

My niece and daughter enjoying a camel ride

One weekend, Michael suggested we take a trip to the Cango Caves, about five hours' drive from Stellenbosch, and we happily agreed. Halfway there, Mona noticed a billboard advertising bungee jumping. Both she and my daughter got excited, asking if we could stop for a few minutes to check it out.

When we arrived, we saw a large crane parked by the roadside. At the top was a platform where you could climb up, tie yourself to a rope, and leap over 100 feet down toward a small river below. Mona immediately expressed her desire to try bungee jumping, if I agreed, of course.

I first brushed it off, thinking she was joking. But when she insisted, I quickly denied her request. "I'm not in favor," I said. Upset by my immediate refusal, she asked why. I gave her the following explanation: "First, you don't have permission from your parents. Second, like any sport, there's always a risk that something could go wrong, or your body may not handle the shock, which could lead to serious injury. Third, I'm on a U.S. Government assignment, so I have limited time to take care of things other than my work, like attending to you in case something happens. Fourth, you're not covered by health insurance here, and we don't have the funds for major medical procedures. Fifth, the locals mostly speak Afrikaans, which could be difficult in case of an emergency. Finally, I'm not familiar with the area, and driving on the left side of the road is a bit challenging for me."

Clearly frustrated with my concerns, Mona interrupted. "OK, OK, I got it, Uncle." She turned away, her face showing that she was upset by my refusal.

We quickly got back in the car and left the spot. Michael tried to shift the mood by talking about the caves, the long drive ahead, and how hot it could get inside. Everyone, except Michael, stayed silent, pretending to listen, while Mona and my daughter seemed to be lost in their thoughts.

A couple of hours later, we arrived at the caves. By then, the bungee jumping incident had been forgotten, and we were all excited to explore the caves—an adventure that was, for most of us, a first.

After parking, we walked toward the entrance of the caves. We all agreed that an hour would be enough to get a good look inside. The plan was to stay together, but if we got separated for any reason, we would meet back at the entrance in exactly an hour.

Before entering, I told the girls that they had no choice but to stay with me the entire time. The plan worked out well. Though there was plenty to see and explore, we stuck together, or at least stayed close enough to keep an eye on each other. We were free to wander and interact, but we kept a sense of togetherness. There were also guided tours inside, and at times, we tried to listen to the guide or follow the group without joining in. But for the most part, we were on our own, exploring at our own pace.

Everyone seemed to be enjoying themselves, but my wife, Kusam, started to feel uneasy, especially in the narrow, slippery paths where water dripped from the ceiling. When we finally emerged from the caves, she let out a big sigh of relief.

Mona and my daughter having fun inside the Cango caves

After seeing some water on the ground, my wife got too scared to take the next step down

Two days before my time was up to return to the U.S., my replacement, a white Caucasian American man, arrived to take over my assignment. After going over all the details about the job and the people he would be working with, the first question he asked me was if I knew of any Indian restaurants nearby. I was surprised by his question and asked him to repeat it, just in case I had misheard him. He asked again, the same way.

During my six weeks there, my family and I had visited many restaurants, but not once did we go to an Indian restaurant. We had a nice kitchen at home, and my wife loved cooking Indian food herself. I apologized to him for not being helpful, but I couldn't resist asking why, of all foods, he was interested in Indian cuisine. He explained that he was a vegetarian and, in his opinion, Indian vegetarian dishes were the best. He added that normally, he would have researched before coming to South Africa, but despite his efforts, he couldn't find any Indian restaurant in the Cape Town area. We were all intrigued by this and, within a day or so, we managed to find a place for him.

The final day arrived, and with heavy hearts, we said goodbye to Michael's family. It felt like we were leaving behind a close-knit family. The kids were nearly in tears, promising to stay in touch when they grew up. We had all enjoyed ourselves, visiting different places, tasting a variety of foods, and never once feeling like we were far from home. The clementines we had tasted were, without a doubt, among the best, if not the best, we'd ever had.

Nearly twenty-five years later, whenever we go grocery shopping, we still think of the South African clementines and always seek them out before considering other varieties.

The Silk Valley in Beijing, China

As part of my APHIS assignments, I had the opportunity to visit China in 2003. In response to a request from the Chinese government, a team of four officials from APHIS headquarters in Riverdale, MD, was dispatched to review the spread of a disease in the pear production areas, for which Chinese pears had been banned from importation into the U.S. During our visit to the orchards and our discussions with Chinese officials about the phytosanitary measures needed to ensure the pears were disease-free before shipping to the U.S., we also took advantage of our free time to explore places of interest like the Great Wall of China, Tiananmen Square, and other attractions recommended or driven to by the Chinese officials. We bought some souvenirs to bring back home.

On our last day in China, after finishing our official business, my colleagues and I decided to visit Beijing's famous Silk Market, also known as Silk Valley, which happened to be within walking distance from our hotel. We wanted to do some shopping before heading back. The market is known for hosting hundreds of shops, much like a flea market, selling items that looked nice, even though many had fake brand labels, and were much cheaper than similar items in the U.S. Upon seeing us, the shop owners became so excited and aggressive in trying to sell their merchandise that they would often lower prices on the spot, ensuring we would leave their shops with something.

It didn't take long before I realized that my bag was completely full, leaving no room for additional purchases. I decided to leave the market and head back to my hotel. Hardly had I taken a few steps when I heard someone walking behind me. I quickened my pace to create some distance, but the person followed, walking fast and calling out "hello," "hello." Turning around, I saw a young girl in her late twenties, holding some colorful items in her hand, trying to get my attention.

As she got closer, I noticed she was carrying some beautiful scarves and was eager to sell them. She pleaded, "Although these scarves sell for five dollars each in the market, I'll sell you ten scarves for just 20 US dollars. I really need to make a sale."

"Sorry, my baggage is all full, and I can't buy any more," I responded.

She didn't give up, offering me better deals, like five scarves for just 8 USD, then five for 5 USD. I apologized again, explaining I wasn't able to buy.

Still not ready to quit, she insisted, "But I really must sell these. At least buy a few." Finally, I agreed to buy just two scarves, which she happily agreed to sell for 2 USD. We exchanged the items for dollars, and before we parted ways, I asked her why she was selling them so cheaply and whether she was even making any money.

Her answer astonished me. She said, "It's not the money I'm after. I'm just trying to practice speaking English with foreigners and learning some negotiating skills. It's part of an assignment for my Master's degree in English."

I couldn't believe what I had just heard. I asked her again, "Would it be okay if I gave you 10 more dollars, just as a little help toward your studies?"

She smiled but declined, saying it wasn't allowed. "But I really appreciate your time and for talking with me," she added.

As I walked away, I couldn't help but wonder whether it was the silky scarves or the unique approach of the people that had given the market its name, "Silk Market."

The Great Wall of China

Visiting a historical site in Beijing, China with my APHIS colleague

My APHIS colleagues accompanied by China officials visiting pear orchards

Inside view of Silk Market, Beijing, China

Why Did I Retire That Soon?

In the United States, Canada, and many other developed countries, there's no official age limit that dictates when someone must stop working. As long as an individual remains willing, able-bodied, and meets the performance expectations of their employer, they can continue working as long as they wish. Given this flexibility, many of my close friends and colleagues have often asked me the same question: Why did I choose to retire from APHIS so soon, just after turning sixty-six?

Generally speaking, people in the U.S. retire voluntarily once they reach their full retirement age. For some, it's due to declining health. For others, employment conditions, economic reasons, or a mix of personal circumstances prompt that decision. Retirement most often takes place during one's sixties, typically around sixty-six, when individuals qualify for pensions or social security benefits under federal or employer policies.

On the other hand, there are plenty of people who remain in the workforce well into their seventies. Some do so because they haven't yet met retirement eligibility criteria or are waiting to receive maximum social security benefits. Others delay retirement due to difficult domestic situations, financial obligations, or because a spouse is still working or running a business.

In my case, the decision to retire stemmed primarily from health concerns, specifically, a progressive hearing loss in both ears and the onset of a condition called Polymyalgia

Rheumatica (PMR), which made life more challenging not just for me, but also for my wife.

Back in 2012, four years before my retirement, I first noticed trouble with my hearing. On the advice of my primary care physician, I consulted both an ENT specialist and an audiologist. The ENT ruled out any physical blockages or abnormalities, but the audiologist's tests confirmed a significant loss of hearing in my left ear and a moderate loss in the right. Age appeared to be the primary culprit, and the audiologist strongly recommended a custom hearing aid for my right ear.

By end of 2012, things had worsened. While driving to work one morning, I noticed that my car wasn't accelerating properly despite pressing the pedal. Fortunately, I was close to work and managed to exit the freeway and park. As I got out of the car, I realized my balance was off. My legs felt unsteady, and I had to hold onto the door to avoid falling. A coworker happened to arrive around the same time and helped me inside to receive medical attention.

Later, my audiologist diagnosed the incident as a mild case of vertigo. She explained that changes in the fluid inside my left inner ear likely disrupted my nervous system, causing the dizzy spell. She prescribed medication to take during future episodes and encouraged me to perform certain vertigo-related exercises regularly. Around this time, I also began to experience a constant ringing in my left ear, tinnitus, which further aggravated my condition.

Based on my symptoms, the audiologist suspected Meniere's disease. To manage it, she prescribed a specialized set of hearing aids known as Contralateral Routing of Signals (CROS). The idea was to place two interconnected devices in my ears so that the left ear would transmit sounds to the right, where they could be amplified and interpreted.

Unfortunately, the solution was only partially effective. While the hearing aid in my right ear worked reasonably well, the one in the left ear transmitted distorted audio, voices tangled with the overwhelming ringing from the tinnitus. It felt like trying to hear someone talk while standing beside the roaring Canadian side of Niagara Falls. Worse, it created the illusion that voices coming from my left were actually on my right, causing me to turn my head in the wrong direction. Eventually, I gave up on the left ear aid entirely and relied solely on the right ear, accepting whatever limited hearing it still offered.

Even with the best technology available, I never regained a normal level of hearing. I often had to ask people to repeat themselves, sometimes more than once, and still couldn't understand them. That recurring frustration made me the target of embarrassment, ridicule, or occasional irritation from others. It was during that season that I began consulting with my HR department, asking about my retirement options and the earliest opportunity I had to step away.

Then, on January 7, 2016, something hit me hard, Poly Myalgia Rheumatica. PMR is an inflammatory disorder tied to the nerves, causing deep muscle pain and stiffness, especially around the shoulders, neck, and hips, though it can spread beyond. That day, the pain engulfed my entire body, leaving me temporarily paralyzed. I had to be rushed to the emergency room at the nearest hospital.

Blood tests revealed elevated levels of two key inflammation markers: CRP (C-Reactive Protein) and ESR (Erythrocyte Sedimentation Rate). The physician on duty looked at me gravely and said, "We're not entirely sure what triggered the inflammation or this level of pain, but fortunately, there's a treatment that works well. It's a steroid called Prednisone. I'll be prescribing it, and you'll likely need to take it daily for at least a year, possibly longer."

She went on to explain the expected side effects: an increase in blood sugar, steady weight gain, and the need for ongoing monitoring. I'd need to work closely with my primary care doctor and a rheumatologist, who might also adjust the dosage as the condition evolved. Ironically, I wasn't the only one "on fire." Just nine days earlier, on December 29, 2015, one of my cars quite literally caught fire.

It was early morning when someone from the neighborhood rang the bell and knocked on the front door, shouting, "Your car is on fire!" I had fallen asleep in my study, only a few steps from the driveway where the car sat. But because I wasn't wearing my hearing aids, I heard nothing. My wife, however, happened to be in the garage at the time and rushed towards me after hearing the man outside.

She shook me awake. Still groggy, I went to the window and saw our SUV, a Kia Sorento, engulfed in flames right in our driveway. As I opened the door, the man explained he had been driving by on his way to work when he spotted the fire. He had already called the local Fire and Rescue Department.

Immediately, my wife and I rushed to connect the garden hose and began spraying water on the fire. Within minutes, emergency responders from the Fire and Rescue Department and the police had arrived. The fire marshal quickly ordered us to step away from the burning vehicle, warning, "You're lucky. The fire was just a minute or two away from reaching the gas tank. No telling what could've happened to you or your house if it had."

The SUV, our Kia Sorento, was completely destroyed. The fire department deemed it unsafe to drive, and later it was towed away by a contractor from our insurance company. I was left without a car.

I called my supervisor to explain the situation, my recent PMR diagnosis and now the loss of our vehicle. She responded with unexpected kindness, allowing me to work from home indefinitely, until I felt strong enough to return in person.

But the blows kept coming.

Just as I was trying to navigate life with a debilitating illness and no transportation, I was struck by a vicious flu. I lost my voice entirely. It was hard to say what was more frustrating, my physical pain or the barrage of calls from the insurance company, each one pressing for details about the car fire. They wanted to know everything: whether anyone had been injured, if other property was damaged, if I suspected foul play. The questions seemed endless.

Since I could barely speak, I asked each caller to send me an email instead so I could respond in writing. Most obliged, but one claim adjuster insisted on going through everything over the phone. I strained to answer him for nearly an hour. At the end of the call, he told me I'd be receiving additional forms in the mail, dozens of them, to be filled out and returned promptly. When I asked if my policy covered a rental car in the meantime, he said I'd have to wait for an answer.

It was a deeply trying time. I could hardly sit, sleep, walk, or talk. With only one car left, one my wife needed daily for work, I had to make do. I dropped her off each morning, worked from home, ran necessary errands, picked up my prescriptions, and then picked her up at the end of the day.

Then came the snowstorm.

Heavy snow blanketed the area, turning roads into icy traps. Travel times doubled, even tripled. I remember one night in particular, took me over three hours to drive a distance that normally would've taken less than thirty minutes. Only one lane on the three-lane highway was open, and traffic barely crawled along.

My wife was equally worn out. She worried constantly about my health and safety, especially given the condition of my legs. I dreaded getting into any accident, even a minor one. If I had to step out of the car, I wasn't sure I could stand.

We considered other option, hiring a taxi, subletting a small place near her work, but with her low business income, neither option seemed feasible. We also looked into hiring temporary help at the store, but the logistics and training demands made it impractical. If things got worse, we were prepared to shut the business down for a few days.

One small relief was that my rheumatologist didn't restrict me from driving. He left the decision to me, which allowed some flexibility. And after about a month, I began to feel stronger, little by little.

My auto insurance company, meanwhile, still hadn't figured out what to do with my burnt car, whether it would be repaired, what they'd pay if it was declared a total loss, or even whether my policy included a rental provision, which they ultimately denied anyway. I could have taken them to court over the delay, the low valuation of the vehicle, and the denial of a rental, but with so many other complications demanding my attention, I let it go. Later, when it came time to renew, I simply switched to another company.

Although my supervisor at APHIS had graciously allowed me to work from home for as long as I needed, I felt uneasy staying away while my colleagues showed up to the office each day. So, about a month after the PMR diagnosis, and shortly after I managed to purchase another car in February 2016, I decided to return to work, even though I hadn't fully recovered physically.

Over the next two months, the steroids significantly reduced the PMR-related pain and allowed me to walk again, though at a slower pace. However, their side effect, a sharp spike in my blood sugar, presented another major hurdle. During my follow-up appointments, my primary care physician recommended I start regular insulin injections, which I could either receive in person or learn to administer myself through a video consultation.

"If that's not something you're comfortable with," she added, "you'll have to maintain your fasting blood sugar below 200. If you can manage that, we can control it with Glipizide instead."

Unwilling to begin insulin therapy, I chose the harder route: strict sugar control. She warned it would be difficult, though not impossible. From that moment, I eliminated anything with even a gram of sugar from my diet, reading every label carefully. I also began monitoring my blood sugar three times a day and emailed her my readings each week.

To her surprise, within two weeks my fasting sugar levels had dropped below 200, despite the high-dose Prednisone. She agreed to put me on the maximum dose of Glipizide, and insulin was no longer necessary.

My next concern was the potential weight gain often caused by Prednisone. But contrary to expectation, my weight actually dropped due to the sugar-free, high-protein diet I had adopted so rigorously. This prompted my doctor to advise supplementing my meals with more meats and eggs to prevent further weight loss.

It ultimately took me a full year to bring my CRP and ESR protein levels back within the normal range. That meant I had to maintain my strict dietary regimen for a whole year, thankfully, just a year.

Although both my PCP and rheumatologist were cautiously optimistic that the pain and inflammation would subside within a year, they were honest enough to admit that in some cases it could take up to five years, or, rarely, even longer. While the timeline was uncertain, the assurance of eventual recovery kept me grounded. The one person more worried than me, however, was my wife, Kusam.

I had already spoken with her about the mounting challenges, my worsening hearing loss, the car fire, the PMR diagnosis, the strict diet and resulting weight loss, and she had every reason to be concerned. The long delay from our auto insurance company regarding our SUV only added to the stress.

All of this led me to think more seriously about retirement. I was only a few months away from turning 66, the age at which I'd be eligible for full pension and Social Security benefits. We still had our business on the side for supplemental income, and we had built a solid retirement savings. It all added up to one conclusion: we could manage.

After more than 24 years with APHIS, I made the decision to retire. When I informed my supervisor, she was surprised. She urged me to reconsider, reminding me that I still had a year's worth of sick leave and could continue working from home indefinitely. But she also said she would understand if I chose to move on.

Kusam and I were both under immense pressure, and retirement felt like the only sensible option. I thanked my supervisor for her kindness and support, but confirmed that my decision was final. My last day on the job would be April 30, 2016.

Chapter V – Surprises Seldom Stop

GBS? What the Heck is It?

O n February 29, 2020, as the world was just beginning to grapple with the onslaught of the COVID-19 virus, a novel coronavirus associated with respiratory tract infections and rising death tolls—I was hit by another life-threatening illness: Guillain-Barré Syndrome (GBS). This rare neurological disorder would land me in the hospital for over three months, including 23 days in the intensive care unit.

GBS is an autoimmune disease in which the body's immune system mistakenly attacks its own peripheral nervous system. It often follows a respiratory or gastrointestinal infection, triggered when certain bacterial or viral components mimic the body's nerve cells, confusing the immune response. Though it can affect anyone, it's more commonly seen in older adults.

In my case, the attack came swiftly and with devastating force. I was completely paralyzed, confined to bed, unable to move anything but my eyes and head. A ventilator tube was inserted to assist my breathing, making it impossible to speak, eat or drink. For two weeks, my daughter interpreted my eye movements and subtle head shakes for the hospital staff, translating my basic needs and responses. But when the

COVID-19 lockdown was enforced, even that fragile line of communication disappeared.

For months afterward, I lived in silence. If I was hungry, in pain, or simply restless, I had no way to let anyone know. I couldn't press a button or call for help. I simply had to endure, hoping someone might notice something in the data streaming across their monitors or follow their scheduled rounds with care.

Gradually, as my body began to recover, my oxygen levels improved. With the support of nurses who gently cradled my head to prevent it from falling, I could sit upright, first for seconds, then minutes. Though tubes still connected me to machines for feeding, urination, and breathing, progress came in small, hard-won steps. The breathing tube was eventually replaced with a less invasive apparatus, which in time was removed entirely. Speech therapy followed, and I slowly regained my voice, just two to three hours of strained speech a day at first.

The hospital provided iPads to allow limited conversations with my family, who were still not allowed to visit due to the ongoing lockdown. Even something as ordinary as a shower remained out of reach. When I begged for one, a senior nurse explained gently but firmly, "You're already immunocompromised. We just can't risk exposing you to the virus." So, I went for months without a proper bath, caught in a strange limbo, recovering from one disease while shielded from another.

Eventually, I was able to transition from liquid nutrition to soft foods, and finally to solids. Each shift felt like a milestone, a small but tangible reminder that I was inching my way back toward life.

But despite everything, my weight, which was about thirty pounds under, remained in the critical zone around 125 lbs. and refused to budge, no matter what or how they fed me. I suspected one reason was their complete restriction of salt, an essential electrolyte. When I questioned this, they told me it was a hospital-wide policy for patients with high blood pressure. I asked to see a published study justifying that policy, but my request was never answered.

Three and a half months after being admitted, still mostly bedridden, too weak to stand or walk, and still weighing only 127 lbs, the hospital staff informed me that I was being discharged. I protested. I was in no condition to go home. But my objections were dismissed, apparently overruled by the insurance company. Despite my repeated appeals, the nursing facility could not extend my stay. The staff explained that the insurer, following US Medicare directives, would not cover anything beyond the standard 90-day period.

Too weak to be moved in any other way, I was placed on a stretcher and sent home by ambulance. Though several skilled professionals, physical therapist, occupational therapist, speech therapist, certified nurse, and nurse aide, visited once a week for the next two to three months, the burden of care fell mostly on my family. My daughter administered insulin shots twice a day. The feeding and urinary tubes remained attached, and it was my loved ones who cleaned and managed them around the clock.

I know how fortunate I was to have my family by my side in that desperate hour. Their presence was life-giving.

It took another six months, along with multiple visits to doctors and specialists, many of which I made strapped to a stretcher in an ambulance, before I could shed the tubes that had become an extension of my body. Eventually, I was able to handle most basic routines again, with help from a wheelchair or occasional family support.

The removal of those tubes brought immense mental relief, especially the catheter. It had required constant attention, emptying the sac every few hours, cleaning, and replacing the entire system from time to time. The discomfort and the sense of dependency were difficult to bear.

Now, more than four years later, I feel mostly cured. But I still live with the aftereffects: weakness in my legs and feet, hearing loss, memory lapses. From stretcher to wheelchair to walking cane, I'm finally back on my feet. Aside from a few falls in the early months, I've mostly been free from GBS-related ailments like vertigo, though the risk still lingers.

Last but not least, I have no doubt in my mind: it was the prayers and well-wishes of my relatives, friends, and community that carried me through the brink of death and placed me, one step at a time, back on track.

Why Did You Move to Virginia?"

I admit that of all the things I disliked in life, freezing winter weather topped the list, and it definitely played a part in my decision of where to settle after retirement. My aversion to the cold had little to do with the fact that I was born and raised in parts of India where the temperature rarely dipped below freezing. Truthfully, I disliked the intense heat of Indian summers too, especially from May through September, but not with the same depth of resentment I felt for the bone-chilling winters of Canada and the northern United States. It was in those frozen places where I encountered some of the most life-threatening challenges I had ever faced, dangers I had never known in warmer climates.

I still recall one night in Winnipeg, Canada, when the winter was especially cruel. I was heading home after a party. It was well past midnight, and the temperature had plunged to nearly minus 40 degrees Celsius. All day, the radio had warned listeners not to remain outside for more than five minutes, cautioning of the risk of freezing to death. That night, my car stalled on the roadside. Later I learned that the antifreeze in the engine had frozen, making it impossible for the car to run.

As I stood outside, my bare hand extended in the frigid air, hoping for someone to stop and help, fear crept in. The streets were nearly deserted, and each passing second felt heavier than the last. I began praying, quietly but desperately. Just as my hope began to wane, a kind driver finally pulled over and gave me a ride. I sometimes wonder if he realized that he may have saved my life.

Another chilling experience occurred a few years later in New Jersey. It was another bitterly cold night, with the temperature well below freezing, and I was on my way home after finishing a work assignment about 70 miles away. Once again, my car failed. This time, the radio announced that due to multiple roadside incidents, emergency services would be delayed by at least an hour. I knew I couldn't wait that long.

Then I remembered a nearby post office just off Route 130 South, the same one where I often stopped to drop off mail on my way to and from work. It had a small lobby with 24-hour access so customers could check their mail at any time. I decided to run for it. The distance was about a mile and a half, and though the cold bit through every layer, I managed to reach the building in about ten minutes. To my relief, the door was unlocked and the interior was warm.

Not long after I arrived, a customer came in to check his mailbox. As he turned to leave, I approached him and explained my situation. By a stroke of luck, and maybe a touch of grace, his route home passed near mine, and he kindly offered me a ride.

Yet another life-threatening experience occurred in the mid-nineties. As part of my work assignment, I was asked to board a cargo ship scheduled to dock at Port Elizabeth, New Jersey, around 2:00 a.m. As a Plant Protection and Quarantine Officer with the United States Department of Agriculture, my responsibility was to inspect specific areas of the ship, including walk-in freezers where fruits, vegetables, frozen meats, and other goods were stored, any of which could harbor exotic plant or animal pests.

Since most of the crew was either asleep or off-duty at that hour, no one accompanied me during the inspection. That was standard protocol.

After completing my inspection inside the freezer, I turned to exit, only to discover that the door had shut behind me. It was designed that way, to maintain the sub-zero temperature inside. But this time, the interior handle, meant to allow someone to open the door from the inside, was missing. The only ways the freezer could be opened were either by propping the door open with an object or having someone outside to assist.

I tried pushing the door open a few times, but it didn't move. It felt like it was sealed shut. I yelled and pounded on the door, but no one heard me, likely due to the freezer's soundproofing. And in those days, I didn't have a cell phone. Panic began to set in. The cold was creeping in fast, and I knew I might have only ten to fifteen minutes to escape before losing consciousness.

In a last-ditch effort, I kicked the door with every ounce of strength I could summon. To my amazement and relief, the door gave way and swung open. It wasn't the lock that had trapped me, but a thick buildup of ice along the doorframe and handle that had frozen the mechanism shut. The ice, ironically, saved my life as it had prevented a complete seal and allowed me just enough gap to break through with force.

That incident left a lasting impression. It led to new safety protocols at our workplace to ensure that no one would ever again be trapped in such a dangerous situation.

These harrowing experiences were always in the back of my mind when considering where to retire. A warmer climate, where I wouldn't have to fear freezing roads or dangerous temperatures, became a priority.

After retiring from my job with APHIS in 2016, we began seriously contemplating a move south. But there were obstacles, the biggest being my wife's shipping business in Silver Spring, Maryland. It was thriving, and we couldn't just walk away. Selling it became our top priority.

Interestingly, after I began helping with the operations, business picked up significantly. This uptick seemed like a good signal, it might be the right time to sell. So, in July 2019, we reached out to a business broker to evaluate the store and set a fair asking price.

Our plan was to first offer the business to our employees, who had earlier expressed interest in buying it. We were willing to offer them a price below the market value if they acted before it was publicly listed.

To our surprise, everything moved quickly. On August 2, 2019, the business was sold. While we were pleased with the outcome, the speed of the transaction caught us off guard. Instead of months, the entire process, evaluation to closing, took just two to three weeks. By August 11, we were out of the store.

The bittersweet part was that neither of us was emotionally ready to step into full retirement. It felt sudden, almost abrupt. But in hindsight, it seemed like a divine hand was guiding the process. Just a few months later, the COVID-19 pandemic would descend, shutting down countless businesses. We had exited just in time.

Towards the end of 2020, just six months after we had sold our shipping business, I was struck by GBS. The illness drastically changed our lives, coinciding with the global shift brought on by COVID-19. As difficult as that season was, we found ourselves repeatedly thanking God. We were no longer burdened with the daily grind of running a business or making frequent store runs, especially from a hospital bed where I lay unable to move, write, or speak for months.

The onset of GBS only strengthened our resolve to move. Our three-level colonial home no longer made sense for my physical condition. With all the bathrooms and bedrooms located either upstairs or downstairs, and no full bath on the main level, simple tasks like bathing became difficult and risky. I couldn't go up or down the stairs without assistance, and even then, each attempt felt precarious.

We realized that aging in place in a multi-level home was not a practical plan. As much as we loved our neighborhood, we needed a one-level living arrangement. At first, we considered renovating our existing home, perhaps converting part of the main floor into a bedroom and full bath. But after reviewing the cost and feasibility, we had to let go of that idea. So we began searching for a new home, one that offered single-level living, fewer maintenance demands, and, if possible, warmer weather than Germantown, Maryland, where we had lived for 21 years.

Finding such a home turned out to be more challenging than we had imagined. The market was red hot, and rambler-style houses that fit our criteria were rare. Bidding wars were common. Buyers were waiving inspections and offering well above asking prices, something we weren't comfortable doing.

After months of looking, we finally found a home that met all our needs. The only downside: it was located outside the area we had originally considered, Manassas, Virginia. Still, we felt we had little choice. We purchased the home and moved within a few months. One major reason for our urgency was that we didn't want to miss the opportunity to sell our Germantown home while the market was still active and before winter, when real estate activity typically slows.

While some friends and family, including our daughter and others living in Virginia, welcomed our relocation, others were less enthusiastic. Many of our relatives in Maryland and members of the Sangat at Guru Gobind Singh Foundation Gurdwara in Rockville expressed disappointment. This was the Gurdwara we had faithfully attended every Friday and Sunday. We had done Sewa there, voluntary service, and built a strong community. Their concern was understandable. Manassas was over 60 miles away, and the distance made regular visits more difficult.

We still make trips back, though not as often as before. And whenever we do, the same questions inevitably come up.

"Why did you move to Virginia?" "What would it take to bring you back?" "Did you know we've started a petition to get you to move back to Maryland?"

I can understand their sentiment. I had served on the Gurdwara board for more than ten years, four of those as chairman. Like all board members, it was voluntary and selfless work, and during that time, I came to know nearly everyone in the congregation. My wife also enjoyed her involvement with the community. She formed close friendships through her service. So, when we announced we were moving, many were genuinely shocked.

Whenever I'm asked about our decision, I offer the same response: it was God's will. And if He ever leads us to move back, we will follow. Still, not everyone accepts that answer. Some insist it was our decision alone, not divine direction. They joke, "We're going to find a place and make you come back."

Even now, more than three years later, this conversation continues every time we visit.

On the hind side, over the past three years, we have looked over thousands and thousands of properties closer to the Gurdwara, yet none has come across that would fit our bill. There will always be at least one thing or the other that would fall outside our selection criteria and make us go back to square one. But the search goes on even today.

Sally

Prior to my retirement in 2016, one weekday morning around 7 a.m., I received an unexpected phone call. The ring was so sharp and sudden that it felt more like an alarm than a call, and I hurried to pick up.

"Inder Paul, are you busy? When do you think you can come to my home and fix my TV?"

The voice was unmistakable, it was Sally, my wife's elder sister. She lived not far from my office in Riverdale, Maryland.

Although my core work hours were from 10 a.m. to 3 p.m., we had the flexibility to start as early as 6 and leave any time after 3. Most of the staff came in around 9, but I preferred to start early. I had always been an early riser, and with the roads quieter before rush hour, I could begin working in peace. That schedule suited me well, I'd usually complete my most important tasks before meetings and colleagues began filling in.

So when the phone rang that early, it shook me. It was rare for anyone to call at that hour unless something serious had happened.

I spoke softly. "Sally, I'm already at work and a bit tied up this morning. But what's wrong with your TV?"

"No channels are coming on. I think something's wrong with the Dish signal. Do you think you can come by later, or should I call someone else?"

She sounded unusually desperate, the kind of insistence that told me this wasn't just about missing a program, this was a matter of comfort, routine, perhaps even company.

"I have a couple of meetings coming up," I said. "But I'll try to take some time around lunch and stop by. Can you manage until then? Are you okay otherwise?"

"Yes, I'm fine, it's just the TV. I've got some important shows coming up today and wanted to make sure everything's working. I can wait till noon. Please don't forget," she said, and then hung up.

Sally wasn't her official name. Her given name was Azaad Kumari. Born in 1948 to a Punjabi Hindu family, just a year after India gained independence, her parents named her with purpose. Azaad meant "free" or "independent," and Kumari, "princess." It wasn't just a name, it was a declaration, and Sally lived up to it in every sense.

Fair-skinned and striking as a child, her mother would often place a black mark on her cheek to guard her from the evil eye. If she cried for long, her mother would burn red peppers over a fire pit to ward off any harm believed to come from envious gazes.

Physically strong and never one to back down, Sally's voice often carried louder than those around her. She didn't just stand her ground, she confronted anyone who dared threaten her or her family. She didn't run to adults or wait for someone else to handle things. If someone in the neighborhood acted up, she handled it herself, and not gently. It wasn't uncommon for the same person she scolded or even thrashed to later show up at her house, complaining to her parents about her behavior.

Sally had seven siblings, six sisters and one brother, and all except one were older than her. True to her nature, she often acted on impulse, speaking her mind or taking decisive action before considering the consequences. Her family, like many others, had endured immense hardship after migrating from what became Pakistan during the Partition in 1947. Sally's younger sister would be born later in 1956, well after the family had begun to rebuild their life in a new land.

The early years were difficult. Her parents struggled to make ends meet, and the constant pressure at home left a mark on Sally. She grew restless, always searching for a way out of the constraints she had grown up with. That chance finally arrived when she turned twenty. Having just completed her Junior Basic Training (JBT), a marriage proposal came from a Punjabi man living abroad. He was older and not well-educated, but what mattered most to Sally was his residency in the United Kingdom and the promise of a new life overseas. Her parents were hesitant; they hoped for a more educated match. But when they saw how determined Sally was, they reluctantly gave their blessing. Not long after, she was married, and in 1970, she moved to the UK.

Thirteen years passed. By 1983, Sally and her husband had two children, a son and a daughter. That was the year I met her for the first time, when she and her family came to attend my wedding to her younger sister, Kusam, who had immigrated to the United States the year before. After the wedding, Sally and her family visited us in Detroit and stayed for a few days. It was during that time I discovered her lighthearted, infectious personality. She was cheerful, full of energy, and often the first to make jokes at her own expense, just to make others laugh. Her knowledge of Bollywood films and dramas was unmatched. Everyone in the family treated her like a walking encyclopedia of Indian cinema.

Several years later, Sally and her family immigrated to the United States when their green card application was approved. In 1990, they moved to New Jersey in search of a business opportunity. That same year, they invited us to join them. We, too, were searching for a new venture and soon relocated from Michigan to be near them. From that point on, our lives became more intertwined, and we grew closer over the next forty years.

Sally had a magnetic presence. No matter who else was in the room, she somehow became the center of attention. Her absence at any party or gathering was deeply felt. She loved playing cards, buying lottery tickets, and taking trips to the casino. Her joy for life was evident in all she did.

Sally at Taj Mahal Casino -1

As the years went by, Sally gradually put on weight, which made it increasingly difficult for her to move around with ease or complete everyday tasks. Even walking a few blocks became burdensome for her, something she tried to avoid whenever possible. To make things a bit easier on herself, she developed a habit of keeping her front door unlocked until bedtime so she wouldn't have to get up each time one came by to visit.

Sally at Taj Mahal Casino -2

Sally's idea of a walk for exercise was charmingly unconventional. She would lace up her shoes, step outside, and sit on the bench placed in her front yard. There, she'd spend fifteen to twenty minutes enjoying the view, greeting neighbors, and soaking in the sun. Then, once her "walk" was done, she would get up and head right back inside. This lighthearted approach to fitness was typical of her, and when she wasn't making jokes at her own expense to entertain others, she often left lasting impressions through other small but memorable moments in her life.

Nothing like cold beer

I think it was in 1988 when Sally visited our convenience store in Michigan. Before moving to the United States, she had owned a similar shop in England, but this might have been her first visit to a store like ours in America. Along with the usual groceries, dairy, meats, and soft drinks, we also carried beer and wine, stored in a walk-in cooler with glass doors for easy browsing.

When Sally saw the cold beverages behind the glass, she looked genuinely surprised. In England, she explained, it was unusual to keep beer so cold. I told her that Americans preferred it that way and suggested she try one. As if she'd just been waiting for someone to offer, she dashed to the cooler, grabbed a bottle, and eagerly took a sip. One beer quickly turned into another, and before long, she was grinning from ear to ear, declaring that there was no need to go home, she could happily spend the entire day sitting in our store, drinking cold beer and wine.

"I like this one, let's buy it."

When it came to big decisions, buying a house, new furniture, planning a vacation, or even purchasing a car, Sally often turned to me for help. Her impatience made it hard for her to wait even a few days, and she trusted me more than others in the family to help her navigate the details.

One day, she called and said she wanted to buy a car over the upcoming weekend. She gave me the basics, her preferred color and how much she could put down, and left the rest to me. I researched a few listings in the newspaper and online, selected some options that matched her preferences, and made a plan.

After picking her up, I briefed her on our approach before heading to the dealership. "Just give me a signal if you like a car," I told her, "but try not to show too much excitement until we negotiate the price. There's plenty of room to bargain."

She gave me a knowing look and replied, "Yes, I know. I'm not crazy, am I?"

As we pulled into the dealership, I shared with the salesman what we were looking for, basic preferences like color, size, and budget, along with a few cars I'd seen advertised in the paper. Whether by coincidence or sheer experience, the salesman led us straight to a car parked nearby and began highlighting its features.

He had barely said a few words when Sally suddenly turned to me and said, loud enough for him to hear, "Inderpaul, I like this one, let's buy it." I shot her a quick glance, trying to signal her to stay quiet, remembering our pre-discussed strategy about not showing interest too early, but she either didn't catch the hint or chose to ignore it. She repeated, even more decisively this time, "I really like this one. I have enough for the down payment, let's just get it. We don't need to see any more."

Turning calmly to the salesman, I said, "Alright, let's see if this one fits within our budget. If not, we might take a look at a few others."

Three hours later, Sally was holding a thick stack of paperwork and a new set of car keys in her hand. Mission accomplished.

"Lightning with no visible clouds in the sky!"

One sunny weekend afternoon, shortly after finishing her shopping, Sally called me in a mild panic.

"Inder Paul," she said, "just a few minutes ago, while I was driving home, I saw lightning. But it was a clear day, bright sun, not a cloud in the sky. How can that happen?"

I paused. For a moment, I was puzzled too. Then suddenly, it clicked.

"I think I know what happened," I said, trying to keep my voice even. "Just wait a couple of weeks, and you'll probably find out for yourself."

But Sally wasn't having it. "What? No! Tell me now. What was it?"

I laughed softly and explained, "What you saw wasn't lightning. It was likely the flash from a speed camera. There's one installed on that road near your house. I noticed it the last time we visited. If you were driving at least twelve miles over the limit, it probably took a picture of your license plate."

She gasped. "Oh God!" And before I could say more, she hung up.

Sure enough, two weeks later, Sally called me back, not surprised anymore. "You were right," she said. "The ticket came in the mail."

"Don't put that in your mouth"

One evening, at Sally's invitation, my wife and I arrived at her home, where a small group of guests had already gathered. Everyone was settled comfortably in a large family room, chatting and waiting for us to join. On the center table, Sally had laid out an assortment of snacks: cooked sausage pieces, breaded fish, and some vegetarian items for those who preferred non-meat options.

As soon as we walked in, Sally shouted with her usual energy, "Inder Paul, come in here, everyone's waiting!" Then, turning to my wife Kusam, she added, "Can you grab some drinks from the fridge and bring them in?"

Before Kusam could move and I could step fully into the room, Sally caught a glimpse of Raju, one of the guests already seated near the food, lifting a piece of breaded fish to his mouth with a fork.

"Raju, stop!" she yelled, startling everyone. "That fish is for Inder Paul. He doesn't eat the other meat, and that's all the fish I have!"

Looking sheepish, Raju put the fish back on the plate. "Sally," he said with a half-smile, "next time, don't put the fish out until Inder Paul ji has had his share."

The room erupted in light laughter, the kind that follows when an awkward moment becomes just another story to retell later.

Where to Buy a Lottery Ticket

Of all the things Sally did with passion and persistence, buying lottery tickets topped the list. It was her daily ritual, she made sure to get her fill of instant scratch-offs and machine-drawn tickets, no matter what.

Her husband often voiced his disapproval. Others, too, tried convincing her that it was a waste of money. But she never budged. "Everyone spends money on entertainment or vacations," she would say. "What's wrong if I spend a fraction of that on my one hobby? You can't win millions unless you have at least one ticket."

And when she did win, even a modest $50 or so, she made sure everyone knew about it. "See?" she'd say triumphantly, "I don't always lose."

So devoted was she to her habit that if she couldn't go out to buy tickets herself, she would call someone else to do it for her. In her later years, when she became bedridden due to serious health issues, she managed to convince hospital nurses to pick them up for her. She even once told a nurse, "You have a job because people like me are here. I'm paying you to take care of my needs, this is one of them."

One day, as she was driving slowly along the highway, so slowly, in fact, that she was far below the speed limit, a police officer took notice. Normally, drivers get pulled over for speeding, but in this case, her unusually slow pace raised suspicion.

The officer approached her car and asked, "Ma'am, is everything alright? Do you know why I stopped you?"

Sally didn't even let him finish. "Officer," she said, cutting in politely but firmly, "before you give me a citation, can you tell me where I can buy a lottery ticket? I've been looking for a shop around here, but I don't know who sells them."

The officer paused for a moment, then smiled. "I know a place," he said. "Just follow me."

To everyone's shock, after a brief illness, Sally passed away in December of 2022. Her sudden departure left a void among those who knew her well and cherished her bold, unfiltered nature. Her presence had a way of lighting up any room, and without her, even card games lost their charm. Few people played after she was gone.

Leap Years and Me – What's Next!

Every January 1st, people around the world welcome the new year in their own way. Like many others, I would join in the celebration, enjoying the day off from work, attending festive parties, watching the ball drop in New York either on TV or in person, taking part in religious programs at the Gurdwara, and sharing warm greetings with family and friends. But beyond the celebrations, I never really assigned much meaning to the day. No resolutions, no rituals, no special sentiments. The year 2024 seemed no different at first glance.

But being a leap year, it stirred something in me. Not superstition, exactly, but a strange sense of reflection.

I grew up in India, a country where superstitions thread through the social fabric, touching nearly every aspect of life—what day you're born, who you marry, whether or not you eat eggs on a Tuesday. Even the way people looked at you could be seen as an omen. There was an old man in our village, a Baba, whom many avoided because they believed he had an "evil eye." These kinds of beliefs were everywhere, impossible to escape.

Thankfully, my parents were different. They didn't believe in such things and raised my siblings and me with the same healthy skepticism. Still, superstitions tend to follow you, even across borders. After moving to the United States, I found that others in my life, my wife, my in-laws, still held on to certain beliefs. Often, I would quietly go along with them, more out of respect than conviction.

233

This leap year, though, brought a subtle discomfort I couldn't ignore. A quiet voice reminding me that in past leap years, things hadn't always gone well.

Back in 2008, during the financial crisis, I lost nearly 40% of my savings. Like many others, I had invested heavily in the stock market, particularly in high-risk Thrift Savings Plan (TSP) mutual funds like C and S. The collapse of the real estate and banking sectors sent everything into a downward spiral.

I remember those days vividly. The fear was real. Sleep became elusive as I played out worst-case scenarios in my mind. Would the markets recover? Would I lose everything? Would I be forced to work for the rest of my life because I couldn't retire? The panic wasn't just mine, everyone around me seemed to be spiraling.

Yet somehow, I managed to hold still. Just a few years before, I'd taken some investment training that proved invaluable. I remembered the core advice: Don't panic. Don't sell when the market is bleeding.

So I didn't. I stayed put.

I even found myself guiding others. One of my senior colleagues, who had once been my supervisor, came to me in distress. She knew about my training and asked what she should do. I told her plainly, "If I were you, I wouldn't touch anything right now." And I meant it.

The following day, she didn't come to work. Two days later, when she finally returned, I asked if everything was alright, if she had been feeling unwell. She smiled and said that she and her husband had gone to see their financial planner. Then, with a teasing grin, she asked, "Can you guess what the advisor told us?" I didn't respond, just watched her, curiosity rising in my eyes. "Exactly what you said," she continued. "Don't touch the funds at this time." I couldn't help but smile. Her words reassured me. From that day on, the nerves began to settle, and I started sleeping better at night. As it turned out, the market did recover over the next two years. Our savings eventually climbed back to where they were before the crash. I had made it through. My nerve breakdown had healed.

But in 2012, I was hit by another one, this time, quite literally.

It was an ordinary morning. I left home early, driving my four-year-old Hyundai Elantra along the interstate toward my workplace in Riverdale, Maryland. Just a few miles short of my destination, I felt the car slow down, far below the flow of traffic. Pressing the accelerator did nothing. I managed, somehow, to pull into the office parking lot.

When I stepped out of the car, I could barely stand. The ground seemed to tilt beneath me, and I nearly collapsed. I clung to the car door for support. Just then, a woman who worked in the same building pulled into a nearby spot. She must've seen the trouble on my face, because she rushed over and steadied me.

"You're having vertigo," she said gently. She helped me inside, where the building nurse gave me first aid.

Later that day, I visited my physician, who referred me to an audiologist. After running tests, the audiologist confirmed what she believed was an episode of Meniere's Disease, a disorder of the inner ear, likely triggered by another nervous system breakdown. She explained that Meniere's is characterized by vertigo, tinnitus, and hearing loss. No known cause, just symptoms that come and go. In my case, it was the left ear that had gone silent. An audiogram confirmed I had lost all hearing on that side.

She prescribed medication to manage future episodes and recommended exercises that simulate vertigo to help retrain my nervous system. After a year of medication and regular practice, the episodes gradually subsided.

Then, on January 7, 2016, I was struck again, this time by something called Polymyalgia Rheumatica (PMR), another autoimmune inflammatory disorder, much like Meniere's. It began with aches and stiffness in my shoulders, neck, arms, hips, and thighs. At its worst, I could barely move. Blood tests showed drastically elevated levels of CRP and ESR, markers for serious inflammation.

The diagnosis was clear. Steroids were the only way forward. I was warned that recovery could take more than a year, and in some cases, the disease could even prove fatal. Thankfully, I responded well to treatment, and within a year, the symptoms had mostly resolved.

Fast forward to 2020, and I faced yet another life-threatening nerve attack, this time, from an autoimmune disease called Guillain-Barré Syndrome (GBS). Like the conditions I had battled before, GBS is largely diagnosed based on symptoms, with no known specific cause or etiology. The doctors initially gave me just a ten percent chance of survival.

My limbs felt like giant blocks of stone. I couldn't speak a single word. Except for my eyes and head, my entire body was paralyzed. Yet, once again, God was on my side. Against all odds, I pulled through. Now, more than four years later, I would say I've recovered about ninety-five percent.

Looking back at these major events, 2008, 2012, 2016, and 2020, I couldn't help but notice some unsettling patterns. Each year had been a leap year. Each had involved a nerve-related breakdown. None had a known cause. All were diagnosed by symptoms alone. And all took about a year or more for me to recover.

So when 2024 arrived, yet another leap year, I found myself wondering what might lie ahead. I wasn't trying to be superstitious, but I couldn't ignore the pattern. "Could there be something in my system that's cyclical? Something that flares up every four years, coincidentally always in a leap year?" The thought looped in my mind, until my wife's voice interrupted me.

"What are you thinking? Are you lost in something again?" she asked, her voice pulling me back into the present.

I shook my head, rubbed my eyes, and told her everything I had been reflecting on, the strange timing of my illnesses, the pattern I had seen unfold over the past sixteen years. As I finished, I noticed her quietly wiping away tears. Without saying a word, she stood up and walked away, disappearing into the room where she usually does her morning and evening prayers.

I realized then that I may have said too much. "Maybe I shouldn't have mentioned that every time I got seriously ill, it was during a leap year," I thought. My attempt to reason through the coincidence had only stirred fear in her heart. My words had disrupted her peace, made her anxious about what 2024 might bring.

"It's just a coincidence…" I tried to say, but she was already gone.

Superstition, I realized, has a way of sneaking back into our lives, especially when we're vulnerable. And sometimes, it doesn't take much to awaken it in someone who had long since let it go.